Star
Principals:
Serving Children
in Poverty

Star Principals: Serving Children in Poverty

Martin Haberman
Distinguished Professor of Education
University of Wisconsin—Milwaukee

Kappa Delta Pi, International Honor Society in Education
Indianapolis, Indiana
1999

Direct all inquiries to the Director of Publications,
Kappa Delta Pi, 3707 Woodview Trace, Indianapolis, Indiana 46268-1158.

Project Editors:	Grant E. Mabie
	Nicholas Drake
Editorial Assistants:	Patti L. Cox
	Tim Tate
Art Director:	Karen L. Klutzke
Text and Cover Design:	Angela Bruntlett

Library of Congress Cataloging-in-Publication Data

Haberman, Martin.
    Star principals: Serving children in poverty/Martin Haberman. p. cm.
    Includes bibliographical references and index.

    ISBN 0-912099-28-3 (pbk.) $18.00

    1. School principals—United States Case studies. 2. Educational leadership—
    United States Case studies. 3. Urban schools—United States—Sociological aspects
    Case studies. 4. School management and organization—United States Case studies.
    I. Title.

LB2831.92.H33 1999

371.2'012'0973—dc21

99-27901

CIP

Printed in the United States of America
99   00   01   02   03   5   4   3   2

Portions of pages 1–13 and 94 are adapted from M. Haberman and G. W. Bracey. 1997.
The anti-learning curriculum of urban schools, Part 1: The problem. *Kappa Delta Pi Record* 33(3): 88–89;
M. Haberman. 1997. Unemployment training: The ideology of nonwork learned in urban schools.
Phi Delta Kappan 78(7): 499–503; and M. Haberman. 1999. The anti-learning curriculum
of urban schools, Part 2: The solution. *Kappa Delta Pi Record* 35(2): 71–74.

Pages 49–53 are adapted from M. Haberman and V. S. Dill. 1995.
Commitment to violence among teenagers in poverty. *Kappa Delta Pi Record* 31(4): 148–56.

Call Kappa Delta Pi International Headquarters (800-284-3167),
or visit KDP On-line (*www.kdp.org*) to order.
Quantity discounts for more than 20 copies.   KDP Order Code 511

Dedication

To Delia Stafford, whose courage, persistence, and knowledge
provide children in poverty with the teachers and principals they deserve.
Her distinctive accomplishments in the selection of talented educators
for all our children has proven to be a major contribution
to improving the quality of public education in the United States.

Table of Contents

Table of Contents

Kappa Delta Pi, International Honor
Society in Education, was founded in 1911. Dedicated to scholarship
and excellence in education, the Society promotes
among its intergenerational membership of
educators the development and dissemina-
tion of worthy educational ideas and practices, enhances the continuous growth and
leadership of its diverse membership, fosters
inquiry and reflection of significant educational issues, and maintains a high degree of
professional fellowship.

Key to the fulfillment of this mission is the Society's publications
program. Kappa Delta Pi's journals, newsletters, books, and booklets
address a wide range of issues of interest to educators at all stages of
the profession.

The Haberman Educational Foundation was started

in 1994 to extend the research and concepts of Martin Haberman, Distinguished Professor of Education at the University of Wisconsin—Milwaukee. The Foundation works to help school districts that serve children and youth in poverty to:

- improve the quality of beginning teachers;
- recruit more African-American and Hispanic teachers and individuals from all cultural groups;
- develop programs to "grow their own teachers";
- bring new constituencies into teaching;
- improve the quality of beginning principals; and
- work with schools and colleges of education to develop programs for preparing teachers and principals for schools in low-income communities.

The Foundation attempts to meet these goals in a variety of ways. By training personnel directors and university faculty engaged in selection to use the Urban Teacher Selection Interview and the Urban Principal Selection Interview, the Foundation has helped to identify thousands of teachers now serving children and youth in poverty. These interviews are used in more than 20 U.S. cities and in Australia, New Zealand, Israel, and Russia. The Foundation also offers free and low-cost consulting services and training to schools.

The Haberman Foundation is devoted to improving the schooling of children and youth in poverty by selecting and preparing more effective teachers and principals. We can best achieve this goal by extending the research and developmental efforts that are daily increasing the number of effective urban educators. For further information, or to inquire about our services, please contact us at:

 The Haberman Educational Foundation
4131 Martinshire
Houston, TX 77025

or call 1-800-667-6185.

Introduction

Being a star means more than being effective. In every major school system, there are substantial numbers of highly effective principals and teachers. Many more are effective to some degree—that is, their behaviors can be connected to the achievement of at least some of the school's stated objectives.

"Star" is a term I started to use in my studies of outstanding teachers (Haberman 1995). Star teachers can be effective even in debilitating situations. In the thick bureaucracies characterizing the 120 largest school systems in the United States, innumerable conditions work against teachers. School bureaucracies are nonfunctional. Teachers face overly large classes, insufficient materials and equipment, endless rules and regulations, and piles of paperwork. In every major school district, there is a group of teachers—approximately 8 percent—who will be effective in spite of the horrendous obstacles the system places in their way. A star teacher can even be effective in a failing school. I contrasted the behaviors and ideology of these star teachers with the behavior and ideology of quitter and failure teachers—typically more than 30 percent of the faculty—who are teaching in the same schools. My studies demonstrate the distinctive qualities of the stars as the explanation for their effectiveness in spite of debilitating work conditions.

In this volume, I use "star" to indicate the behaviors and ideology of principals who are more than effective. There are no effective urban school districts. All large school systems are failing to some substantial degree. Yet, within every one of these school districts, there are highly effective schools. The principals of these schools succeed in spite of the bureaucratic conditions set in motion against them by the states and school districts in which they must operate.

The attributes of star principals, which make them effective against all odds and in spite of irrational pressures, are more than behaviors. They are behaviors undergirded by an ideology. The ideology and the behaviors are interwoven; they are of a piece. The connection between what star principals do and how they think about what they do cannot be broken. In other words, educators who believe they can learn the "magic" behaviors without having the belief system that goes with it are wasting their time.

Conversely, those who would assume that, because they agree with the ideology, they can automatically perform as star principals are equally deluded. Star principals are doers and thinkers.

The basic assumption of this book is that training individuals to learn this ideology is essentially a waste of time. Potential star principals must first be selected. That is, individuals who already hold the ideology that characterizes star principals can benefit from subsequent training and learn the effective behaviors. For those who do not espouse the ideology, the behavioral training will result in a hollow and ritualistic performance without commitment and understanding. I do not mean to imply that individuals cannot be trained to become stars; rather, star training will only "take" with individuals who already accept and are committed to the ideology. The ideology is a value-laden system of beliefs *caught* and developed by life experiences rather than *taught* in graduate courses of school administration.

This gap between ideology and the real world explains much of the stress principals experience in schools serving children in poverty.

The instrument I recommend school districts use for selecting star urban principals— one many urban school districts already use—is *The Haberman Urban Principal Selection Interview.* Chapters 2 through 12 of this book mirror the concepts assessed by the interview. Each chapter represents one function of leadership vital to the performance of an effective urban principal. The ideology of star principals is interspersed throughout the following cases and analyses. A few highlights of this ideology are summarized as follows:

The Ideology of Star Principals

★ For any real learning to occur, the safety and security of everyone in and around the school building is an absolute prerequisite.

★ Teachers are not here to help me be a principal. I am here to help them improve students' learning.

★ To improve the learning of impovished students, students and their families must be connected to health and human services.

★ I am paid more than teachers not because I am smarter, work harder, am the best educator, or hold a state license as an administrator. I am paid more because I am accountable and responsible for the effectiveness of the total school.

★ Teachers who can control their classes are not necessarily good teachers. Classroom management is a necessary but insufficient condition. Student learning is the criterion for deciding teachers' "goodness."

★ Parents are not the consumers of education; society is. The role of parents is not simply to have things explained to them. Parents are sources of useful information about their children, resources in the educational process, and partners in meeting the needs of students.

★ Everyone who sets foot in this school must be treated as if he or she were an important dignitary.

★ Leadership means helping people demand what is in their best interests rather than acceding to whatever they want.

★ Admitting shortcomings of the school program is the first step toward resolving weaknesses; I must never stonewall or cover up.

★ There is no greater benefit to the school than removing an ineffectual teacher. No matter how lengthy, costly, or time-consuming the process, it must be pursued to completion.

★ To be accountable for instruction, I must be involved in the selection and assignment of new teachers.

★ There is nothing of any importance that I can decide completely on my own.

★ It is my job to protect this school from the chaos in which we must operate. Despite state mandates, school board politics, temporary superintendents, and central office turf wars, I can keep this school focused on the kids and their educational needs.

Appointing School Principals

In contrast to the ideology of star principals is the process by which they are appointed. The attributes of star principals do not necessarily coincide with the qualities superintendents and school boards seek when making appointments. Star principals must have excellent communication skills and be extremely sensitive to the needs of their school communities. These attributes may actually be used in the hiring process. In the real world, however, politics, ethnic background, and personal idiosyncracies will likely be considered in making appointments. This gap between ideology and the real world explains much of the stress principals experience in schools serving children in poverty. The star principal has a set of deep commitments but is likely to be appointed for other reasons. It is fortunate—and somewhat surprising—that this unaligned process between the school system's stated goals and the process it follows in hiring new principals still produces a substantial number of star principals.

In urban districts, the superintendent has the strongest voice in making final principal selections, but others have input—and the school board has final approval. The real-world criteria used to appoint principals, in order of importance, are:

1. **Control.** Will this individual be able to control and manage the building? Safety, order, and a controlled environment are imperative. Urban schools are safe havens in neighborhoods frequently characterized by violence. If the principal cannot manage the building, he or she must be removed. There is no other choice.

2. **Loyalty.** The second criterion used in making the selection is whether the appointing official sees the candidate as "one of my people"—or someone who will become "one of my people." The principal's role is viewed as a political one that must support the system as well as the superintendent who makes the appointment. The superintendent appoints principals who will represent the system downward to teachers, staff, parents, and community. The principal is not appointed to advocate upward, representing what teachers and parents want to do to change the system. This dilemma causes the principal great stress. There is, however, no conflict in the mind of the superintendent making the appointment: clearly, he or she will appoint the loyal soldier. Granted, the principal is expected to listen empathetically and even respond when he or she can to the requests of subordinates. Nonetheless,

advocates for restructuring the system, activist representatives of the community, or risk-takers seeking to make radical changes cannot meet this criterion.

3. **Insulation.** The third criterion is an extension and synthesis of the first two. The job of subordinates—in this case, the principal—is to resolve problems before they reach higher levels of administration. Principals ineffective at containing problems and engaging in damage control allow school problems to reach the central office and the superintendent. The superintendent does not have time to resolve a particular school's problems with parents, safety, discipline, or curriculum. If the principal engenders or elicits union grievances and lawsuits, he or she becomes an albatross to the superintendent, who has a full agenda of his or her own. The job of the principal is not like that of the matador who waves the bull past and lets him plow into the central office. The superintendent sees the principal as confusing, deflecting, or killing the bull. The good principal "keeps trouble from my door." This concept of insulation operates at all levels. Principals, for example, identify good teachers as those who do not send kids to the office, evoke parental complaints, or make serious demands.

4. **Educational Leader.** If the superintendent views the principal candidate as someone who can keep a lid on the building, support the boss, and protect the system from potential complaints and demands, he or she can now consider the degree to which school achievement can be raised and dropouts kept in school. The rationale for ranking the school's major purpose fourth is the belief that these volatile problems must be solved at the building level because the superintendent must deal with too many sites to manage them personally. This position is certainly understandable. The problem it presents in the real world, however, is that many individuals who can meet the first three criteria frequently cannot meet the fourth—and vice versa. In fact, the number of principal candidates who can meet all four criteria is likely to remain low enough to keep the need for effective urban school principals at a level we might term "desperate." This fact is especially true when we consider the fifth criterion.

5. **Communication.** Superintendents seek principals who can represent the school system to parents, teachers, staff, students, business leaders, the unions, community agencies, church leaders, and, most of all, to the various ethnic constituencies the school serves. This criterion requires oral and written communication skills that are complex, highly developed, and extremely flexible. The principal who meets this criterion listens to all constituencies interacting with the school. Because they will perceive such a principal as someone representing their views and desires, he or she may be able to enlist constituents in resolving the most pressing problems in ways that are best for both the clients *and* the system. This criterion, however, can be a source of stress for the principal. The instances in which urban principals can make important changes by simultaneously representing a constituent need and protecting the system from too much change are infrequent. The communicative proficiency that effective principals need is similar to that of a government ambassador. The best interests of parents and their children are frequently at odds with the best interests of the school system. Most decisions are made to protect and enhance the system rather than the children. The star principal communicates so well that he or she is able to enlist teachers, students, parents, and community members in support of district policies.

We can select individuals who share the star ideology and predict that they will express this ideology in their own distinctive ways.

There are, of course, notable exceptions in which superintendents' main criterion in choosing administrators is what is best for the children. Hal Guthrie, Superintendent of Texas's Spring Branch Independent School District, hires star principals such as Janna Mahaffey because he understands the ultimate values he and his principals must preserve for children. In the long run, his success will be judged on whether his schools raise student achievement rather than who wins school political values.

Clifford Janey, Superintendent of New York's Rochester City School

District, may be the best urban school superintendent in the United States. He selects administrators for their ability to overcome rather than feed the school bureaucracy. Dr. Janey actively supports school principals like Willie Buck of Rochester's Martin Luther King School (#9) for putting kids' needs ahead of the system's. When the school's achievement scores increased, Buck delivered on his promise to dance the Macarena (with parents) in front of the entire school population.

The following chapters outline the ideological crisis permeating most urban schools in the United States. Chapters 2 through 12 focus on the various roles of urban principals in trying to meet the needs of teachers, students, and the community. Each of these chapters features a case study and analysis. These chapters conclude with discussion questions suitable for preservice and in-service teachers and administrators.

As the following chapters will show, we need not clone individuals such as Mahaffey and Buck to find other star principals. We can select individuals who share the star ideology and predict that they will express this ideology in their own distinctive ways.

Chapter 1

The Ideology of Unemployment

Urban schools fail to reach students because principals, teachers, and staff members teach values of failure.

For many urban youth in poverty, moving from school to work is about as likely as having a career in the National Basketball Association. Though urban schools often struggle and fail at teaching basic skills, they are typically quite effective at teaching skills that predispose youth to fail in the world of work. The urban school environment spreads a dangerous ideology of behaviors and beliefs. This philosophy "works" for youngsters by enabling them to get through urban middle and secondary schools. Yet the very ideology that helps young people slip and slide through school becomes the source of their subsequent failure. Easily learned, readily implemented, rewarded by teachers and principals, and supported by policies, schools promulgate this belief system because it is easier to accede to students' street values than to shape them into more gentle human beings. The latter requires a great deal of persistent effort, not unlike a dike working against an unyielding sea. It is much easier for urban schools to lower their expectations and simply survive with youth than it is to try to change them.

The ideology of unemployment ensures that those infected with it will be unable to enter or remain in the world of work without serious, in-depth unlearning and retraining. Many urban young people are not just ill-prepared for work; they are systematically and carefully trained to be quitters, failures, and the discouraged workers who no longer even want to seek employment. It is almost counterproductive to help urban schools do better at what they now do. They are a basic cause of the hopelessness and desperation characterizing their graduates' lives.

The dropout problem among urban youth—as catastrophic as it can be—is less detrimental than this active training for unemployment (Downey 1993). In effect, urban schools create a pool of young people—much larger than the number of dropouts—labeled "successful" but more carefully schooled for failure.

Chapter 1

Educational Values

That the unemployment ideology is not a formal part of the stated curriculum does not make urban schools any less accountable for its transmission. Anti-work learnings are absorbed as students participate in and interact with school policies, administrators, teachers, safety aides, and other school staff members. Much has been debated on the values taught in schools. Yet many seem oblivious to schools' actual values. The following outline offers a brief description of the beliefs and behaviors comprising this unemployment ideology.

Nowness

What is the unit of learning time in your classes? In urban schools, learning is typically offered in disconnected jolts. In the worst scenarios, no one connects the day's work with the work of preceding days or subsequent ones. Life in most urban schools is comprised of specific periods and discrete days, each of which is forced to stand on its own. If students do not complete homework or take books home—universal behaviors for most males and many females, especially after the elementary grades—everything they are taught must be compressed into isolated periods or "stand alone" days. Teachers, principals, and students survive one day at a time.

By focusing on what can be learned during one period or activity, educators claim to "meet the needs of students" who are frequently absent and would always be playing catch-up. Indeed, some urban schools have classes with more than 100 percent turnover between September and June. Another rationale for this disjointed curriculum is the number of pull-out and special programs legitimizing youngsters missing classes. Still, the most common reason offered for teaching "nowness" is that students seldom remember anything they have been taught. The introduction of any new concept or skill inevitably requires an extensive review of everything that might have preceded the concept. For example, an eighth-grade teacher tries to give a lesson on election results. He or she quickly discovers that most of the class cannot explain the difference between the city, county, state, or federal levels of government. The teacher can either back up and spend the period trying to teach these distinctions or offer the election lesson to the few who might understand it. Some young people have learned to "play dumb" to keep teachers from ever offering their planned lessons. In most cases, however, students are genuinely ignorant of the most elementary concepts that teachers must assume they know to offer the required curriculum.

Nowness is the operating norm of the urban school. A successful period or activity is one in which students prepare nothing and pursue nothing subsequently.

In the absence of connections with what students already have been taught—several times—and already should know, and with little certainty that students will remember today's lesson tomorrow, much of what goes on in urban classrooms resembles daytime television: brief, jejune activities generating a superficial passing interest but requiring no real involvement. One can tune in to a program—even one based on knowledge, such as *Jeopardy*—on any day, without falling behind schedule. There are always new words, so viewers need not remember the previous day's words. Best of all, the rules are quickly given anew each day. The person who tunes in for the first time knows as much as the person who has been watching every day. Anyone can show up and play the game.

Teachers promulgate nowness because, like their students, they are simply trying to get through each day with the least hassle. Yet, if nowness controls the conditions of learning, there is no way to learn any ideas of any consequence or develop skills to any high level of proficiency. Education is a process of building connections, and this process means hard work for students and even harder work for teachers. By "going with the flow," teachers and schools support students' misconception that the unit of time in which anything can be taught and learned is less than one hour. What kind of job can be learned in this amount of time?

Showing Up

What is the minimum standard of satisfactory work at your school? "The deal" in urban schools refers to a tacit working agreement between students and teachers. The student does not disrupt the class; in return, the teacher ignores his or her inactivity. School attendance is thus transformed from passive existence into a virtue. Being there is all that matters. Work is not expected; teachers ask merely for the absence of negative behavior. Teachers purchase this peace with a passing grade of "D-" to answer the student who says, "If I never showed up, I would get an 'F'. I showed up. I deserve better." By passing students for just being there, school policies and teacher behaviors systematically teach young people that existence is an action. In effect, students learn that, if they do nothing bad, they deserve some type of reward. Though attendance is a necessary condition for learning, it is not a sufficient condition. By rewarding inaction, uninvolvement, and a detached presence, urban schools promulgate the dangerous and destructive myth that the minimum standard for "doing" satisfactory work is attendance. What kind of job can be performed through mere attendance?

Chapter 1

Make Me

Who is accountable for what your students learn? Urban schools are conducted as authoritarian institutions. Principals are not replaced because their students fail to learn; instead, they are ejected when the building is out of control. The need for safety from the surrounding neighborhood as well as the need to create an internally safe environment are certainly understandable and desirable. Unfortunately, this perceived need for authoritarianism also controls how the curriculum and learning environment are shaped. Urban youth believe that the principal, teachers, and staff run everything; that school is essentially "their deal, not ours." They see endless rules, a prescribed curriculum, and the pedagogy of poverty. This directive pedagogy supports students' perception that their learning is the teacher's job and responsibility. Students describe good teachers as the ones "that made me learn."

By allowing—indeed, rewarding—students for being passive witnesses, schools support student perceptions that all relationships are essentially authoritarian rather than mutual. As young people see the world, they are compelled to go to school and teachers get paid to be there. Therefore, it is the job of the teacher to make them learn. Every school policy and instructional decision that does not involve students spreads the virus that principals and teachers rather than students must be the constituency held accountable for learning. In a very real sense, students are being logical. In an authoritarian, top-down system with no voice for anyone at the bottom, why should those "being done to" be held accountable? Who would keep employees who believe that it is the boss's job to make them work?

Excuses

How often can your students be late or absent and still make passing grades? Of all the unemployment values urban schools teach, they teach this one best. Students believe they can be late or absent as much as they want, provided they have a good excuse, someone's permission, or a written note. Lessons taught or missed are of little or no consequence. What matters is the quality of one's excuse. If one has valid excuses, there is no limit to the number of "excused" latenesses or absences a student may have and still be "passing." The value says, "If it's not your fault you are absent, then it's as good as being there." And "being there" passes.

In a recent survey, urban middle school students responded to the question, "How many times can you be late or absent in a month and hold a regular job?" More than half the students responded that you could be late as often as you had a good excuse. Almost half responded that you could be absent any time you had a good excuse. In discussions about their responses, no urban youngster has ever suggested that students bear the responsibility of making up for missed work—or even finding out what was missed. If the issue of missed work is raised, students respond with the validity of their excuses. It is beyond the realm of their consideration to deal with the issue of the missed work itself. If reviewing missed work is raised as a direct question—"How do you learn what you missed?"—students typically respond, "Review is what teachers do." Is it possible to hold a job by showing up when you feel like it?

Noncooperation

Should your students have to work with people they do not like? Urban youth typically respond to differences with their peers by threatening or using force. Any body language or verbal interaction is brief and merely an initial preface to the escalation process. The value students bring to school is one of "might makes right." Indeed, "might" is the only determinant of "right." Schools seek to teach nonviolent options, such as peer mediation, and even engage in negative reinforcements as a consequence of overtly aggressive behavior. Despite the large number of suspensions, expulsions, and other authoritarian school responses, teachers and principals do not deal with most students' day-to-day behavior in terms of detention or suspension. The response to students' inability to coexist peacefully is to separate potential combatants. If disputants were not separated, urban schools might resemble a war zone or the floor of the Roman Coliseum. Efforts by urban teachers to use cooperative learning require heroic, consistent efforts to contravene the street values students bring to school. It is easier and therefore more common for principals, teachers, and safety aides to separate students than to teach them how to get along with one another.

Students come to expect segregation from rivals as a way to prevent fighting. They do not practice peaceful coexistence or improved communication as an alternative to violence, because they have been taught the street values of power and control. Moreover, the school most likely has done nothing to disprove the efficacy of these values in their daily lives. Teachers and principals cannot be there when students face the everyday situations they encounter outside of schools. Students and their parents believe, therefore, that they must learn to "take care of their own business." The problem is that, *inside* the school building, where educators do control the environment, no systematic training exists regarding alternatives to violence. The easy way out is for educators to pretend that violent behavior remains irreversible in urban youth. Thus, the simplest strategy is the best one: separate potential combatants. The effect of implementing this strategy consistently for 13 years is to reinforce the ideology of noncooperation; that is, you should never have to work with anyone you do not like or with whom you cannot get along.

Respect

On what basis do your students gain or give respect? The naive or uninitiated person might assume that schools teach students to respect those individuals who know a lot, can learn a lot, or at least try hard. In urban schools, these values carry such little weight with students that they are unobservable. Indeed, trying hard or demonstrating initiative is regarded in many schools as a negative—a form of toadying to authority. The basis of gaining or giving respect is power. The critical question is, "Who can do what to whom?" Between the system and the students, as well as among students, the issue is couched as respect for the power to hurt, whether indirectly or directly.

In response to the question, "When is it okay to hit people?" urban middle school youth provided an interesting array of being "dissed"—that is, being disrespected. Included on their list (Haberman and Dill 1995) was "He talked crazy" and "He looked at me funny." Urban youth clearly believe that words or glances perceived as provocative require a physical response. They use being provoked as a justification for retaliating against the offender or escalating the level of conflict.

The issue is not the students' street values per se but how schools reinforce those values rather than teach, or even try to teach, any alternatives. The concept that one "earns" respect by doing good things is unheard of among most urban youth and requires explanation. Respect is a value extended to the powerful and afforded by looking at a person and knowing his or her potential to inflict physical or psychological harm.

School policies and educators who try to respond to young people in terms of power are doomed to failure. There are no legal means for schools to hurt students. Once students reach the age or size when parents can no longer control them, students also perceive the school as powerless. After all, schools can no longer report them and force them to suffer the consequences at home. Once students reach the age when no power consequences can be administered, schools and teachers have no basis for being afforded their respect.

The option open to schools is to refuse to accept the power value and, from the earliest grades upward, never to use it. Only by relating to students and attempting to control their actions through internal and gentle means does the school hold any hope of contravening this power value (Haberman 1994). Granted, it is harder relating to young people on mutual terms rather than from a position of power, but most current policies teach students that school is no different than the street—just less effective. Again, it is all a question of who can do what to whom. Is the power to hurt another person an acceptable basis for giving and gaining respect in the workplace?

Authority

How should your students deal with the people in charge and with the rules? Students' approach to school authority is undergirded by their belief that any system is out to get them. The criminal justice system, the welfare department, health-care providers, and the housing authority are a few of the systems with which families in poverty interact on a continuing basis. Because urban schools relate to students and their families in the same impersonal, controlling, legalistic ways as these other institutions, the "we-they" stance is extended to schools. Students perceive of school as another institution with which they must contend. Combined with the Make Me value ("The teacher is responsible for making me learn") and the Respect value ("You give and get respect on the basis of who has the power to hurt you physically"), this Authority value becomes an especially potent force for preparing young people for a life of nonwork. It is difficult to imagine going far in either a part-time, nonchallenging job or in a professional career by showing that the bosses and the organization are seriously flawed.

The dysfunctional nature of how urban schools teach students to relate to authority begins in kindergarten and continues through the primary grades. With young children, directive teaching that relies on simplistic external rewards still works to control students. As children mature and grow in size, however, they become aware that the school's coercive measures are not really hurtful (as compared to what they must deal with outside of school) and the behavior-modification methods practiced in primary grades lose their power to control. Indeed, school authority becomes counterproductive. From upper elementary grades onward, students know well that school authorities have little power to hurt them. External controls do not give students an internal desire to learn; they teach the reverse. The net effect of this situation is that urban schools teach students in poverty to relate to authority as a kind of game. The deepest, most pervasive learnings resulting from this game are that school authority tries to control them in a toothless manner and that those in authority seem out of touch with students' lives. To urban students, school authority represents "what *they* think *they* must do to keep *their* school running." Students do not identify with the school as "ours." They do not own the rules and regulations; school authorities do. Making the authoritarians look bad or stupid is the operating value. Showing that school rules can be bent or circumvented is a sport. It is also clear that, in this game, the students are winning easily. How well will an employee succeed if his or her goal is to show up the boss and the organization?

Peers

Who are the people your students should care most about pleasing? There is nothing new about the fact that peers are the strongest influence on adolescent behavior. The difference today, however, is the nature of the street values young people bring from the neighborhood into the school. What adults see as irrational or bad behavior is actually quite sensible. If one lives in a violent neighborhood, is learning to take care of oneself less reasonable than reporting violence to authorities? If one is faced by constant attack from several adversaries, is it foolish to be part of a group that offers protection? Urban youth learn that schools cannot really hurt them but other young people can and will. The best protection is to avoid being isolated and alone with no one to look out for you.

Educators expect and assume that they will become the focus of students' "respect." Teachers, principals, and other school staff constantly refer to students' need for role models. Most staff members would like to serve as those models for the young people in their schools. Youngsters, however, extend respect to those who can inflict hurtful consequences and extract respect from those they can hurt. Reporting acts of violence is contravened by students' view that they must ignore authorities, because authority can never be there to stop the violence. There are not sufficient school safety aides and police to protect every youngster all day, every day. Violence is a normal condition of everyday urban living. When students see their peers as the most influential and important people in their lives, violence is a normal response.

It is unlikely that any urban school program or staff can shape, control, or teach its students more than a fraction of what peers do. Typically, this influence focuses on what not to do—e.g., do not carry books, complete homework, take responsibility, prepare, or remember what has been taught. The core of this peer influence is to resist *participating* in middle or high school; students should merely *witness* it. The view is, "Show up to see what they try to get us to do today." Media outlets and educational analysts often focus on the small number of students who act out and challenge authority in overtly aggressive ways, but they ignore the majority of urban youth whose school behavior might best be described as passive resistance. What does responding to peers rather than the system portend for one's subsequent functioning in the world of work?

Messing Up

How often should your students be given another chance? Urban schools pander to the student belief that, no matter how often one does something wrong or neglects to perform an expected behavior, he or she "deserves" another chance. Teachers or principals who do not provide an endless series of chances are defined as "unfair." In extreme cases, the student may be required to look remorseful or even apologize. In no case, however, do students believe *anything* should preclude another chance.

Urban schools pander to the student belief that, no matter how often one does something wrong or neglects to perform an expected behavior, he or she "deserves" another chance.

To counter the charge that they cannot control students and make them learn, urban school administrators adopt strategies to deceive the public. In one strategy, "suspended" students simply choose another school and must be admitted if that school is under their quota. The school system then claims it has a rate of 100 percent nonsuspension when, in fact, they actually have only a lot of student movement. This process is called "the dance of the lemons." Another strategy is to support alternative schools that simply warehouse thousands of "troublemakers." Ostensibly, these youngsters are still being educated and will return to their regular schools. In truth, most of these students are "ghosts"—they disappear but are still carried on the attendance rolls for purposes of state support. Every urban district has thousands of such ghosts; some have tens of thousands (National Center for Education Statistics 1995). If all the ghosts on the books actually showed up, no urban school district would be able to cope without building more schools.

To gain public approval, urban schools become victims of their own overblown promises. They accept the street value that it is their job to *make* students learn rather than to do everything possible to *encourage* them to learn. From there, it is a short step to supporting and enhancing the ideology of always getting another chance. What are the implications of carrying this virus into the world of work?

Explaining Success

How should your students account for doing something well? Urban young-sters asked to explain why they have done something well offer various explana-tions: ability ("I'm just good at that."); luck ("I'm a good guesser."); or connections ("My friend picked me for that."). The explanation cited least is effort. There are several reasons for this. First, students espouse the Nowness value, which precludes effort that connects today with yesterday or tomorrow. Second, and even more important, it is not "cool" to try hard at school activities. If one tries hard and fails, it shows that one is stupid. If one tries hard and succeeds, it shows that one is not as smart as the individual who expends no effort and succeeds. The best an individual can do is to be perfect with no effort or preparation at all.

Teachers frequently misinterpret this facet of student ideology. They assume students do not want to learn when they refuse extra help or resist teachers who try to help them. These rebuttals are especially strong when teachers offer help in front of peers. How much can students learn if they believe they are not supposed to make mistakes in front of peers? How much can young people learn if they pretend, or really believe, that they are supposed to gain knowledge without effort or study? Schools that ignore effort foster this value.

Instruction that does not deem engaging students in active effort as the teacher's highest goal plays into proclivities to see effort as a sign of weakness. Every time a school emphasizes right answers and grades at the expense of persistent effort, it misses teaching achievement and success. In every field of human endeavor, the best explanation of success is effort. Thomas Edison's log indicates that he made approximately 10,000 trials before discovering the tungsten filament for the electric light. As the saying goes, "The difference between coal and diamonds is that diamonds stayed on the job longer." What does learning to reject effort portend for a future "worker," and what does it do to our society?

Relevance

Should your students have to learn things they consider irrelevant? In discus-sions of relevance, ends and means are often confused. Relevance relates to connections between content to be learned and students' life experiences. This concept does not mean teachers should give up trying to teach content beyond the current life experiences of urban youth in poverty. Indeed, the very purpose of education is to push students beyond their present understandings and open their minds and imaginations to the universe of ideas. To do anything less is to lower expectations and standards. Making the content relevant by limiting it to students' experience does not meet student needs; rather, it panders to ignorance. Experience is an important way of knowing and understanding the world. Education adds other ways of knowing to the process of experiencing things directly. Educated people learn from the experiences of others—literature and history, science and research, theories and explanations, imaginative ideas, religion, intuition, the arts, and countless other sources.

When a student learns only that which is presently understandable, he or she becomes a hostage and not a beneficiary of personal experience. The criterion of immediacy should not be used to limit learning. Urban youth in poverty are limited in access to positive role models and life experiences. Genuine relevance must be viewed in terms of helping students live out their futures in neighborhoods and communities yet to be developed.

Purpose

Is it reasonable for students to expect work to be fun? The learning of skills to any advanced and useful degree rarely gets labeled as "fun." Indeed, learning can involve genuine drudgery.

Many urban youth believe good teachers can not only make them learn but also in ways that are fun. Naturally, teachers should strive to make learning as pleasant as possible, yet fun cannot be the ultimate standard for judging the work of teachers. Students frequently must learn hard and complex concepts. Many require memorization, intense concentration, and fatiguing repetition.

If schools accede to and support an ideology that "good learning is always fun," what will they actually teach students about work? Should good feelings come from having fun activities, or should one be taught to feel good by accomplishing goals? If work must be fun, what are the prospects for success in the workplace?

Staying on Task

How often can your students come and go and still be considered "working"? In many urban schools, students come and go all day. Urban schools report 125 classroom interruptions per week (Delgadillo 1992). Announcements, student activity, messengers, safety aides, and intrusions by other staff members account for just some of these interruptions.

It is not unusual for students to stay on task only 5 to 10 minutes every hour (Payne 1984). Textbook companies and curriculum reformers are constantly thwarted by this reality. They sell materials to schools with the assurance that all students will learn a given amount in a set time. They are dismayed to observe that an hour of school time is not an hour of learning time. Observers of life in urban schools have reported that the learning of subject matter is rarely the main activity occurring in these institutions (Lortie 1975). What does the process repeatedly of changing tasks portend for fulfilling a job in the world of work? If schools reinforce the behaviors of coming, going, and being interrupted, for what kind of work will students be equipped?

Ignorance

Who bears the responsibility for knowing the rules? Many schools teach students that the best way to circumvent the rules is not to know them. The value students learn is that one must be informed of rules to be held accountable. Rules must be sent home. Parents are asked to acknowledge that they have read them with a signature. Students who do not learn the rules are taught them again. This practice deems classroom and school rules no different from any other form of learning: "something the teacher is responsible for making me learn."

If this approach to teaching responsibility were not sufficiently counterproductive, the problem becomes compounded when combined with other values, such as Excuses. Teacher: "Why didn't you know you had only five minutes to get to class?" Student: "I was absent the day you explained the rule." Again, what does this learning portend for participating in the world of work? Is ignorance of the law an effective excuse in the real world?

Investment

Whose school is it? Many urban youth are taught that they have no stake in the process of schooling. If the school were to be torn down, it really would not matter, because students would be sent someplace else.

Urban schools communicate the message that students are unnecessary to the process. One of the major differences between star teachers and quitter teachers centers on this point. A star teacher convinces students that they are needed: "We

couldn't do what we need to do in this classroom without your total participation."
Quitter teachers communicate the reverse: "This is my class. If you can't shape up,
I'll suspend you." Is it surprising then that youth taught by quitter teachers have no
investment in the building, the program, or any other aspect of the school? What
message does it send to these future workers if they are trained to believe that the
success of the total organization has nothing to do with them?

Implications for the Future

Urban school graduates who carry the virus of unemployment ideology are
unlikely to get a job or keep one. For an individual infected with this ideology
actually to work, the job would have to be characterized by the following conditions:

1. No screening process exists for getting the job beyond
   showing up.
2. No previous training is required. The job can be explained in a
   few minutes.
3. There is a boss who will watch what you do and see that
   you do it.
4. The boss is always there.
5. The boss is responsible for what you do.
6. You can come and go as much as you want as long as you have a
   good excuse.
7. If you are late or absent, you can begin working again without
   having to make up work or revisit what you missed.
8. You do not have to talk to or work with anyone you do not like.
9. You do not have to listen to anyone but the boss.
10. No preparation is needed to come to work.
11. No one expects you to take any work home.
12. You get paid for the time you spend at work, not for what you
    accomplish.
13. No matter how long you work, the job never changes.
14. You merit a raise based on the length of time you have "worked."
15. You do not really have to respect anyone who cannot hurt you.
16. It will not matter if your employer is successful or the work gets
    done; that is not your problem.
17. It will not matter how many mistakes you make, because you will
    get another chance.

18. The work must be fun.
19. You do not have to remember or follow the work rules if no one tells them to you.
20. You do not have to stay on task more than a few minutes each hour.

Meeting these conditions will limit the type of jobs urban school graduates can get. Any such job will likely be part-time, because staying on task, as well as coming and going, is a problem. The job will be of little importance, because how well tasks are done is not a primary concern. The job will be menial, because there is almost nothing to know. The success of the organization or company will not be tied to worker effort. Before schools can change this unemployment training, they must recognize how they promulgate the process. Only then can schools counter the damage they have done.

Chapter 2

Leadership in Urban Schools

School leadership is the process of putting the best interests of the school's children ahead of the convenience of the adults.

Who does the principal lead? Typically, experts analyze the leadership of the principal as if only teachers were involved. Before examining how principals demonstrate leadership of the faculty, it is important to understand that the principal is the leader of all constituencies working in the school community—including groups that report directly to central-office supervisors. In some systems, for example, custodians report to supervisors in the central office, even on how frequently they empty wastebaskets or change toilet paper. The same might be true for cafeteria workers, whose menus and supplies may be managed centrally. Each school system varies in the degree to which principals actually control all the personnel. School bus drivers believe they work for the company that hires them. Secretaries who have passed civil-service exams may transfer to public-service jobs outside the school system. Part-time psychologists, nurses, and social workers may perceive that they work for the administrator who assigns them to schools. Reading or science specialists may work in the school district only for the duration of a grant. School safety aides may have a central-office superior who can reassign them based on changes in violence patterns. In major urban school districts, questions like "Who reports to whom?" or "Who is your boss?" can become quite difficult, often engendering muddled responses. In practice, however, the principal is responsible and accountable for integrating everything in the building and making it work. As the school leader of all these constituencies, the principal naturally is responsible for students. How the children perceive their leader influences the total school climate.

The general assumption is that the principal is the "boss," commonly defined as someone who exercises authority over others. This assumption of power over school personnel is similar to the assumption of teacher power—that teachers can make children learn. The truth is quite different. Star teachers elicit learning through their abilities to organize, motivate, and communicate. They establish trust and rapport with students and connect with the children's caregivers. They know their content and have clear, high goals. They establish working teams and reward effort rather than ability. They are fair, hard-working, and respectful. They regard their work as creating the conditions under which children will learn. The attributes of star teachers have analogues in the behavior of star principals. Leaders become more effective when they concentrate less on being the boss and more on creating conditions under which school personnel perform their duties with fewer impediments.

Sources of Power

What are the usual explanations of the principal's power? How do these power sources play out in the work of principals in the real world?

The first source of the principal's authority is his or her *legitimate* power. The principal can do these things by virtue of his or her legal standing in the school system. Buried in the central offices of every urban school system are board actions that empower the principal to do specific things in the school. The principal, for example, has the legal authority to assign teachers to particular classrooms and determine the children assigned to a given class. Other powers come from tradition rather than statute. For example, the principal can designate the coach of a school team or make exceptions to school rules. Another form of legitimate authority is determined by teacher contracts. In many districts, principals have their own bargaining units and may even negotiate their own contracts. Thus, the principal's legitimate powers include those derived from school laws governing the district; traditions in the district; contracts between teachers' unions and the district; and contracts between bargaining agents for the principals and the school district. In an increasing number of school systems, staff members other than teachers will also have negotiated union agreements that proscribe the legal powers of the principal.

A second source of the principal's authority derives from *reward* power. What can he or she do for anyone? What can he or she give to anyone? Rewards vary among districts. The assumption here is that the principal can lead by distributing rewards and thereby gain compliance if not support.

The third source of the principal's authority derives from *coercive* power. What can the principal do—without violating his or her legitimate power—to punish noncompliance? The assumption here is that the principal has at his or her disposal powerful negative reinforcers that will control, if not shape, the behavior of others in the school. Among these powers is the principal's ability to give evaluations or reports to others with even greater power to coerce responses.

A fourth source of the principal's authority is his or her *expert* power. Expert power refers to those abilities a principal uses to gain a following among constituencies who can do things for the school. To what extent can the principal use knowledge of subject matter, system politics, or parent and community groups to exert leadership? To what extent can he or she use the ability to speak a foreign language to exert leadership? Some principals are experts in the workings of school bureaucracy, and they use this knowledge to get more for their schools. Indeed, in some urban school districts, one building may receive twice the annual funding of another school because of the principal's political expertise. Principals also demonstrate different abilities and expertise in securing business partnerships that support their schools.

> *The effective leader knows that his or her greatest power is persuasion. The principal's job is difficult and stressful for precisely this reason.*

The fifth source of authority for the principal derives from his or her *personal* power. The principal might be quiet and introspective or highly charismatic. In either case, his or her personal abilities to gain support, or engender aversion, can be a primary and fundamental source for leadership.

The Use of Power

Star principals eschew the use of coercive power. They focus their reward power on providing encouragement. They typically utilize their legal power only as a last resort. The emphasis of star principals is on expert power and personal power. Trying to force ineffective school personnel to perform specific acts leads to hollow forms of compliance—compliance in form but not in spirit. I do not mean, however, that a principal should decide not to require and enforce a teacher's punctuality. Rather, the principal must also use other forms of power to get this teacher to perform effectively after he or she arrives on time.

Star principals focus on creating conditions that will enable their staff to achieve success. Some staff members, however, may no longer seek to be effective, or they may have been job *holders* rather than professionals from their first day in the school. Star principals and less-than-satisfactory principals take different paths. Ineffective leaders resort to their legal power, union contracts, coercion, or bribery. The effective leader knows that his or her greatest power is persuasion. The principal's job is difficult and stressful for precisely this reason. He or she cannot, in reality, force anyone to do anything. Coercion does not elicit the enthusiasm and commitment needed to make performance optimal. When a star principal resorts to legal or coercive power, it is as a last resort; he or she has given up on an individual and seeks to move him or her out of the school. In short, school leadership has two goals: to elicit voluntary commitment to shared purposes, and to create the conditions of work that will enable the staff, teachers, and children to be successful.

Case 1: Everything Is Race

The Alexander Hamilton Middle School is the oldest in the district. It has the lowest achievement levels, the highest truancy, and the greatest teacher turnover.

Bob Smith, an African American, is the new principal. He has replaced an administrator who had served for 24 years. During the first month of his appointment, Smith realizes that the faculty, staff, students, and parents define every issue and problem in racial terms. A strong and constant current of racial tension seethes below the surface of almost every interaction, communication, and decision.

As school leader, Smith realizes that he must address this matter. He cannot join in the pretense that this anger, tension, and stress do not exist. After observing the workings of the school, Smith decides to attack the problem by confronting personnel in the main school office. He sees visitors, parents, and students to the office being treated abruptly and without consideration. Office staff members are especially discourteous to African Americans. Upon further observation, Smith notes that this behavior characterizes the way most staff members interact with visitors, parents, and students. Secretaries are discourteous. Safety aides enforce school rules selectively. Janitors complain only about some of the students. Teachers have disproportionate numbers of students removed from classes or tested for special education.

Smith faces the task of stopping behaviors that foster a racial divisiveness in the school. He must also implement positive actions that will reward staff, students, and parents for engaging in unifying behaviors. Smith understands that this situation is pervasive; it undermines staff morale, the possibility of cooperative professional action, and, ultimately, student achievement. He realizes that the assistant superintendent assigned him to the school to resolve this dilemma.

As Smith learns more about the school community, he sees it as varied and complex. Some parents want to make sure their children are well educated and fairly treated, whereas others are uninvolved and hard to reach. Some parents want to help make school decisions. Others merely seek employment as safety aides or from one of the numerous grants that fund the work of community members in schools. Within all these parent groups are several subgroups at odds with one another. Are some parents receiving different and better treatment than others? This question is a constant source of stress for the principal seeking to reach all parents equitably.

As his first year moves along, Smith perceives that the situation is deteriorating. Constituencies increase their expectations that he, as school leader, should be doing more to resolve the divisiveness. The most discourteous secretaries are pressuring for rules to control parent behavior in the school office. The teachers who remove the most students from their classes are requesting tougher rules related to suspension. The safety aides who apply rules least fairly are requesting a metal detector and video monitors for hallways. Some of the least involved parents are seeking greater voice in school decision making. The undergirding issue always seems to be the same: differential treatment based on race.

Analysis

The larger U.S. society has much the same problem as Hamilton Middle School, but Mr. Smith does not have the luxury of waiting for Supreme Court decisions. As principal, he must change the Hamilton school community and how it perceives and interprets what is happening.

The manner in which Smith analyzes this situation and proposes a course of action is a valid indicator of what he regards as "leadership." Does he resort to legalisms such as job descriptions and contractual agreements? Does he try to work one-on-one with each individual he regards as a problem? Does he meet with small groups representing various constituencies? Does he seek to institute new school-wide rules and policies? Does he think town meetings are a useful process? What does he define as indicators of whether positive objectives are being met? How does he evaluate courses of action? Does he persist in various treatments or flit from one solution to the next? Is everything tried at once? How does Smith demonstrate that he is accountable and responsible for improving this situation?

The first step for Smith will be most time consuming; he must listen. School staff, teachers, and parents will all have stories of how they have been unfairly treated in some previous situation. They will also have ideas of what must be done. Smith must listen with as much empathy as possible, but he must not indicate that he will solve or take care of all the problems presented to him.

After he has listened carefully—and this process may take many weeks—

Smith will have a better idea of which problems might be readily resolved, partially resolved, or in need of longer-term treatments. He will also be able to separate the whiners from the people with legitimate complaints and begin to get an idea of which individuals propose workable ways to solve problems.

What Smith needs to establish credibility are some "stop light" victories— smaller issues that can be resolved quickly, such as equal access to a copying machine, the distribution of materials, or the recognition of some meritorious action. A principal can initiate these simple actions in ways that demonstrate he or she is sensitive to issues of equal treatment. As some of these easier actions are implemented, Smith can select more difficult issues such as how many inclusion students are assigned to each classroom. As Smith moves from easier to more difficult issues, he will establish a track record to which he can point. He will be able to point to an increasing number of decisions made with access and equity in mind. Eventually, the whiners will be regarded as making unfair accusations and those who make positive contributions will be rewarded.

The divisive issue of race is so endemic to our society it may never be fully resolved, but it can be worked on and improved. A star principal recognizes this notion and works to demonstrate fairness in every action and policy.

Discussion Questions

1. Which constituency might Mr. Smith choose first to demonstrate quickly that progress can be made?
2. What are some observable indicators that would show Smith is making progress toward improving race relations in the school?
3. What human and material resources might Smith need to handle this problem in a systematic manner?

Chapter 3

Commitment to Student Learning

The better a teacher is, the more protection he or she will need from the criticisms of those who will feel upstaged and threatened. Providing such support is the kind of problem a star principal enjoys.

Few if any principals are ever appointed because they can give a comprehensive answer to the question "What is good teaching?" Yet, in the role of principal, they are expected not only to know good teaching when they see it but to foster it. There is much common agreement about bad teaching: students are off task; teachers do not offer valuable content; discipline problems interfere with students trying to learn; and student work does not reflect progress in achieving classroom objectives. The teacher who cannot keep students interested or maintain their effort on assigned tasks is readily identified as inadequate. There is not such widespread agreement, however, on the behaviors of good teachers of children in poverty. The indicators most urban principals accept as evidence of satisfactory teaching behavior may even be detrimental to the learning of children in poverty.

The Pedagogy of Poverty

An observer of urban classrooms can find examples of almost every form of pedagogy: direct instruction, cooperative learning, peer tutoring, individualized instruction, computer-assisted learning, behavior modification, student contracts, media-assisted instruction, scientific inquiry, lecture, teacher-led discussion, tutoring by specialists or volunteers, and even problem-solving units common in progressive education. In spite of this broad range of options, there is still a typical form of teaching accepted as basic. Indeed, this basic urban style, which encompasses a body of specific teacher acts, seems to have grown stronger each year since I first noted it while supervising student teachers in Harlem in 1958 (Haberman 1987). Now, as we enter the 21st century, urban schoolteachers who do *not* engage in these basic acts as

Chapter 3

the primary means of instruction would likely be regarded as deviant. In most urban schools, not performing these acts for most of each day would be considered prima facie evidence of not teaching.

I refer to these core functions of urban teachers as the pedagogy of poverty:

★ giving information;
★ asking questions;
★ giving directions;
★ making assignments;
★ monitoring seatwork;
★ reviewing assignments;
★ giving tests;
★ reviewing tests;
★ assigning homework;
★ reviewing homework;
★ settling disputes;
★ punishing noncompliance;
★ marking papers; and
★ giving grades.

This basic menu of urban teacher functions characterizes all levels and subjects. A primary teacher might "give information" by reading a story to children, while a high school teacher might read to the class from a biology textbook. Interestingly, both educators might offer similar reasons for their decisions: "The students can't read for themselves" or "They enjoy it when I read to them." Taken separately, there may be nothing wrong with these activities. There are occasions when any one of these 14 acts might have a beneficial effect. Taken together and performed to the systematic exclusion of other acts, they have become the pedagogical coin of the realm in urban schools. They constitute the pedagogy of poverty—not merely what teachers do and what youngsters expect but also what parents, the community, and the general public assume teaching to be. This urban pedagogy appeals to several constituencies.

First, it appeals to people who did not do well in schools. Those who have failed or done poorly in school do not typically take personal responsibility for such failure. They generally find it easier to believe that they would have succeeded if only somebody had *forced* them to learn. Consequently, they offer little compassion to today's students enduring similar conditions.

Second, the pedagogy of poverty appeals to those who rely on common sense rather than thoughtful analysis. They criticize humane and developmental teaching aimed at educating a free people as mere "permissiveness." To such people, permissiveness is the root cause of today's educational problems.

Third, it appeals to people who fear minorities and the poor. Bigots typically become obsessed with the need for control.

Fourth, those who have low expectations for minorities and the poor also find the pedagogy of poverty appealing. People with limited vision frequently see value in limited and limiting forms of pedagogy. They believe that at-risk students are served best by a directive, controlling pedagogy.

Finally, it appeals to people who do not know the full range of pedagogical options available. This group includes most school administrators, business leaders, and political reformers, as well as many teachers.

Unfortunately, the pedagogy of poverty does not work. Youngsters achieve neither minimum levels of life skills nor what they are capable of learning. The classroom atmosphere created by constant teacher direction and student compliance seethes with passive resentment that sometimes bubbles into overt resistance. Teachers burn out because of the emotional and physical energy they must expend to maintain their authority every hour of every day. The pedagogy of poverty requires that teachers who begin their careers intending to be helpers, models, guides, stimulators, and caring sources of encouragement must transform themselves into directive authoritarians to function in urban schools. Yet people who choose to become teachers do not do so because at some point they decided, "I want to be able to tell people what to do all day and then make them do it!" This gap of expectations and reality means there is a pervasive, fundamental, and irreconcilable difference between the motivation of those who become teachers and the demands of urban teaching.

For reformers who seek higher scores on achievement tests, the pedagogy of poverty is a source of continual frustration. The clear-cut need to "make" students learn is so obviously vital to the common good and to the students themselves that surely—they believe—there must be a way to force students to work hard enough to vindicate the methodology. Simply stated, they act as if it is not the pedagogy that must be fitted to the students but the students who must accept the untouchable method.

In reality, the pedagogy of poverty is not a professional methodology at all. It is not supported by research, theory, or the best practice of superior urban teachers. It is actually a collection of certain ritualistic acts that, much like certain religious ceremonies, have come to be conducted for their intrinsic value rather than to foster learning.

There are those reformers who contend that the pedagogy of poverty would work if only the youngsters accepted it and worked at it. Yet that is precisely the problem. Students in urban schools overwhelmingly *do* accept the pedagogy of poverty, and they *do* work at it! The students' stake in maintaining the pedagogy of poverty is the strongest possible kind: it absolves them of responsibility for learning and puts the burden on the teachers who must be accountable for *making* them learn. Students do not want to trade a system that keeps their teachers responsible for one that makes them accountable for what they learn. It would be risky for students to swap a "Try and make me" system for a "Let's see how hard I can work" system.

Star Principals and Pedagogy

Star principals have an entirely different perception of what good teachers of children in poverty do. They regard generating interest, instilling motivation, and engaging students in learning as the primary function of the teacher. In place of assignment-making and monitoring compliance, these principals help teachers hook students on learning. Whenever teachers can make a learning activity of intrinsic value, it is possible to transform children into genuine learners.

There are a few direct ways in which principals can help their teachers move from using extrinsic rewards with children to generating internal motivation in their students. First, principals must support teachers who use the "project method." This method involves integrating more than one area of subject matter in student-centered projects. This approach is common in primary grades, for example, when children may study and count birds in their natural habitat, read and write stories about them, and then construct models and learn why birds can fly. It becomes less common as children advance through the grades, and the method is almost nonexistent at the high school level. Yet children in poverty learn best when they can see their learning in large, integrated chunks of subject matter rather than as discrete, unrelated specifics. They also learn best when they can apply such integrated learning to life situations. Problem solving and answering questions they regard as meaningful will lead students to higher levels of thinking and understanding.

To foster the project method, principals must do several things. They must protect teachers who may not follow the predetermined classroom textbook page by page. Indeed, there may be clutter, noise, and moving around as children work on projects. Students may need to take more trips outside the school building than do children in other classes. Construction, banging, and hands-on work will transpire. There may be complaints from custodians about extra cleaning. Other teachers might even voice disapproval when they see students develop interest for learning in classes using the project method. In all these instances, it is the job of the principal, first, to recognize real learning when it happens and, second, to protect the teachers and children excited about this type of learning. Inevitably, they will need the principal's protection. If some teachers are unhappily and unsuccessfully going through texts, merely "covering" material and simply trying to enforce the pedagogy of poverty, they are likely to be burning out. Furthermore, their children will be difficult to manage. As these teachers see colleagues happily engaging students and getting young people to work independently, they will feel upstaged—and they will be right. The burned out teachers will pressure the principal to interfere and even stop teachers from using the project method. They will raise "questions and concerns," such as:

★ "Our curriculum committee spent all last year agreeing on a textbook. Is Ms. X following the text?"

★ "There's a lot of noise and confusion in that room."

★ "Are those children being prepared for the achievement tests?"

★ "Parents are unhappy with what's going on in there."

★ "The kids I get from that class aren't getting their basic skills."

It is the job of the principal to protect student learning and the teachers who foster it. Real learning for children in poverty means implementing the project method—not all day in every subject, but for a substantial period of class time. Fortunately, the children who become genuinely involved in learning via this approach will do well on basic skills and achievement tests. In the long term, it is just such accountability that undergirds the principal's support of these teachers.

Real learning for children in poverty means implementing the project method—not all day in every subject, but for a substantial period of class time.

Case 2: Safety Glasses

Laura Carter teaches ninth-grade general science and general mathematics in Bell High School. She is especially focused on her two periods of science each day. Over the past two years, she has completed a master's degree in science education and received several awards for projects completed in her classes.

Carter notes with pride that she uses science to improve her students' reading, writing, and math skills. Student achievement is rising rapidly in her classes, and the children are excited about her projects and learning. Carter is able to build on students' interests and engage them in higher-order thinking activities. By any measure, students in her science classes achieve more than do typical students in the district or in Bell High School.

The key to this type of teaching is hands-on activities. Carter believes strongly that her students do not learn best by only reading textbooks or watching demonstrations—they must actually *experience* science.

Bell High School's district has specific safety rules. All students, for example, must wear safety glasses to engage in science experiments. As a new school, Bell did not receive all the glasses it needed when the school year began. To compound this problem, the district initiated a policy stating that the central office must purchase all glasses and then distribute them to the schools, the purpose being to save money by purchasing in bulk.

The procedure for securing safety glasses requires each science teacher to fill out a form and submit his or her request to the school office. The office accumulates requests and forwards one total request to the district's central office. In September, the central office informed Bell High School that its glasses would be delivered by January—they arrived in April. Each pair of safety glasses cost $12.50; the central office and the school would each pay one-half.

Following this policy caused a good deal of frustration among the teachers as they waited for the glasses to arrive. Until then, no science experiments were to be conducted in their classes.

As part of her social life, Carter met a man in early September who happened to be a dealer in surplus army goods. This man offered her 65 pairs of safety glasses at $1.00 each. Carter purchased the glasses and distributed them to her two science classes. As a result, her students began conducting science experiments while children in the other classes waited for glasses. Carter's students were not only learning more but enjoying themselves. They told their friends, who then complained to their own teachers about their classes being boring: "Why can't we do experiments like the kids in Ms. Carter's class?"

A delegation of teachers soon called upon the Bell High School principal and complained to him about Carter. "We follow the rules and are in effect punished," they argued. "We don't get safety glasses. We have to offer our students a read-about-science curriculum rather than a hands-on curriculum. We have to listen to student complaints about why they can't have Ms. Carter as a teacher." The teachers requested that the principal stop Carter from using the "illegally secured" glasses. If they had to suffer the delays of the bureaucracy, Carter should have to suffer with them. They stated in no uncertain terms that it was a question of fairness. All teachers must be treated alike, and all students must be treated alike. The final comment of the teacher committee was that they expected the principal to resolve this situation quickly.

Analysis

The principal in this case is dealing with more than the issue of safety glasses. The teachers who have come to him are, in effect, arguing that, if most children are not learning as well as they might be, then the few who are learning must also be held back. For these teachers, upholding the school policy for securing safety glasses is a more important value to be preserved than supporting children's learning. Adhering to bureaucratic regulations thus takes precedence over implementing the reason we have schools in the first place—to foster children's learning. Moreover, the manner in which the teachers presented the problem to the principal is "either-or." Either the principal stops the lawbreaker teacher and her children or the principal contributes to a serious breach in maintaining school law and order, thereby making the flouting of school policies an acceptable practice. The complaining teachers are also saying they feel frustrated by the delay in securing safety glasses and would like to be teaching more.

The principal has an important role in resolving this matter. To seize this opportunity for putting all the teachers on the same team rather than on opposing sides, the principal must redefine the problem. First, the question is not, "Do we or do we not get Ms. Carter to stop immediately?" The question is, "How do we share the safety glasses among more students for at least part of the time?" Second, the principal can demonstrate leadership by taking action to speed up the central office procedure for securing glasses. This step would include learning the details of the purchasing process and calling suppliers personally.

Once the number of safety glasses was deemed insufficient by teachers and it was determined that it would take an inordinate amount of time to secure new ones, the principal should have taken inventory. Precisely how many glasses were in the building? Once he reached a count, the principal might have involved teachers in developing a schedule that rearranged their class experiments to share and make the best use of the glasses available. In addition, he could have asked Carter to inquire whether her friend could provide more glasses for everyone at a similarly reduced rate.

Discussion Questions

1. In what ways might the principal have made this a nonproblem in the first place?
2. Which problem should the principal now be most concerned about resolving?
3. Which aspect of this problem is most likely to have lingering effects on the school in the future?

Chapter 4

Theory into Practice

Political leadership produces majorities and minorities; educational leadership produces a shared vision among the school's staff, parents, and community.

There is no shortage of experts stating their versions of what principals must know and what constitutes leadership. Lists of this essential core of administrative knowledge vary in length. They also vary in the sources from which they derive the principles that should guide the work of principals.

Principles of Leadership

Some experts derive their principles of leadership from the field of psychology (Haberman 1982). The assumption is that, because the principal must work through other individuals to reach students, he or she must be an expert at motivating adults—whether by offering support or providing rewards. The key leadership dimensions here include concepts such as motivation, needs, rewards, encouragement, self-understanding, and adult learning. The field of psychology claims aegis over these words and concepts. In this approach, the principles of leadership involve diagnosing the needs and motivations of all the individuals involved in the school enterprise and then providing the appropriate incentives for managing them toward the desired goals.

Other experts derive their principles of leadership from the field of communication (Haberman 1982). Running a school is analyzed and explained as the giving and receiving of messages. Are the messages simple or complex, clear or confused, open or hidden, honest or manipulative? What are the purposes of the forms of communication utilized? What are the effects of the various communications? How can they be improved? This approach focuses on the diverse meanings different constituencies attach to the same situations. Problems are defined as breakdowns in communication: African Americans versus European Americans; men versus women; rich versus poor; and those with political power versus those without voice. In effect, school problems are analyzed in terms of how communication processes can be improved. As in the psychological approach, communications experts assume that if only people understood each other better they would work together better.

A third field producing principles for principals comes from business (Haberman 1982). Business management has extremely clear goals—more sales, lower costs, and more profits—and these are applied to education. These experts substitute student learning for the bottom line, conceive of parents as the consumers, and view professional educators as the sales force. The goal is simple and clear: raise achievement scores. The management style is also clear: run a more effective sales force. The solution for low-achieving schools is to close down operations not producing results.

In addition to psychology, communication, and business, it is possible to analyze a school using concepts from other fields. The field of economics could lead us to ask who profits from this system and the way schools are organized. Political science asks who controls what happens, who makes decisions, and who is disenfranchised. The tenets of history could lead us to ask how this system developed and what forces and trends continue to control the school. Sociology seeks to understand the agreements and conflicts in values among the groups involved. Anthropology asks how the religion, language, and culture of the various ethnic groups affect the school.

All of these knowledge bases for deriving the numerous principles of school leadership are of some partial value. They all offer a few insights that have some validity. Yet none of these approaches explains everything happening in the school community. Even using all of these approaches does not explain everything going on in the management of an urban school.

Educational psychology addresses how people learn in schools rather than in life. Educational economics refers to how people use each other for personal gain in the socialized sector of public education. Educational history refers to trends and great events that have affected schools in years past. These various disciplines, however, have not contributed much useful understanding in explaining or improving school leadership. Experts using these ways of knowing have simply applied them to education and ignored how the institution of the school transforms "learning," "profit," or "culture." In other words, there is no reason to believe that the most effective psychologist, linguist, businessperson, sociologist, anthropologist, economist, historian, or political scientist could be an effective school principal.

Indeed, even a renaissance person who was all of these things would still lack the required principles.

Serving the Constituency

Why are there so many principles of leadership? Why are these principles not more useful? An even more compelling question regarding endless lists of leadership principles: Why is leadership explained in *universal* terms? There is no recognition that administering a public school in a major modern city is *significantly* different from running a school in a small town or suburb—and both will differ from leading a private or religious school. Much like the fallacy of all teachers being universally competent is the assumption that a principal does the same things for the same reasons whether his or her school is in Scarsdale, New York, or the Cabrini Green Housing Project in Chicago. Indeed, it is downright dangerous to contribute to the myth that leaders for schools serving children in poverty can be selected, prepared, and evaluated using supposedly universal principles of educational leadership. A school leader serving a constituency in urban poverty has three basic principles that he or she must adapt to the particular school: unity of purpose, team building, and commitment to task.

Unity of purpose is not readily achieved in an urban school. Although a majority of the students may be at risk of dropping out—behind in basic skills and knowledge, and generally disengaged from the learning process—staff members will offer different explanations for why students are there as well as the school's primary purposes. Most urban teachers have very limited goals for students: Get a job, and stay out of jail. Others, however, will argue that "making decent people" is their primary goal. Still other teachers believe that preparing students for post-secondary institutions is their primary goal. When the discussion is framed in terms of *how* they will realize these goals, many differences arise among school staffs. Some teachers emphasize their particular subject areas as the most effective means of realizing success. Others focus on surveys of business leaders and advocate marketable skills, computer know-how, and behaviors related to keeping a job. A vocal minority of teachers still call for general areas of learning unrelated to any specific subject matters, such as "learning how to learn" and the ability to progress from job to job. When parents' views are solicited, the picture becomes even more muddled. It is easy to call for the principal to achieve unity of purpose but quite another matter for him or her to achieve it. Nevertheless, effective urban principals do tackle this issue, knowing its difficulties and pitfalls full well; however, meetings cannot go on endlessly. Ultimately, a principal must group and prioritize various perceptions of goals. Once that step has been reached, the principal can lead the constituencies to identify the two or three goals that will be the school's highest priorities for the next few years. In addition, school constituencies can identify objectives that support and lead to the agreed-upon goals. For example, a school community can agree that, after three years of bilingual education, students will be capable of functioning in monolingual situations. Participants may also specify several specific objectives to be reached for this transition to occur.

Once the principal has achieved unity of purpose around major goals, he or she can implement the second principle of leadership: team building. Teachers, staff, and parents must work in cooperative ways to achieve the objectives leading to the agreed-upon goals. Procedures of tasks and time periods can be laid out once teams have been organized. This step may sound easy, but it is at this point that personal animosities and philosophical conflicts must be checked.

The third principle of leadership comes into play after individuals have been organized into teams to achieve goals. Commitment to task refers to how the principal will motivate teams to work hard and persist until the goals have been reached.

The most effective school principals translate grand ideas into simple courses of action. By focusing on unity of purpose, team building, and commitment to task, school leaders can turn their action plans into achievable results. What makes these principles special to urban schools is how the leaders implement them in a setting characterized by violence, excessive bureaucracy, racial or ethnic tension, and children who must be helped to overcome the debilitating conditions of poverty.

Case 3: Principal's Pets

Lenora Hagen had been the principal of Garfield Middle School for 15 years. When she was first hired for the position, the school served a population of children from working-class European-American families. Gradually, Hispanic families populated the area. Today, more than 90 percent of students at Garfield are Hispanic. The largest group is of Mexican extraction, yet there are also children from Puerto Rican, Cuban, and Central and South American families. Hagen did not learn any Spanish herself during this period, but she developed a strong bilingual program, hired bilingual teachers and aides, and integrated Hispanic studies throughout the curriculum.

Each year, school achievement continued to slip downward, despite extra support from the central office of the Great Cities School System. A large grant from a national foundation was used at Garfield to involve parents. After implementing a well-funded three-year project, parental involvement was at an all-time high. Still, achievement continued to decline.

Garfield has the highest rate of pregnancy for any middle school in the state. It also has the fewest number of students who go on to high school. Over half of the student population "disappears" after eighth grade. Many never even show up on high school rolls.

The Great Cities school board placed Garfield School on probation five years ago. Hagen realized her career was at stake. One way she responded was by "buying off" potential critics in the community and in the school. She hired community members in every possible way—as safety aides and general school assistants, for instance. She began paying school-parent council members for attending meetings; she also covered expenses for meals, travel, and baby-sitters. By "investing" the school discretionary funds in the community, Hagen developed strong support from influential community leaders. This strategy also worked with parents who had been highly vocal and visible critics of the school. These parents were hired to perform various jobs—real as well as nonexistent—for which they received $10 per hour. Each year, as the superintendent and school board sought to close the school, Hagen was able to marshal her community support, ethnic newspapers, and local politicians to beat back any attempt to replace her or close the school. Each year for the past five years the central office has had to cover up to $200,000 of expenditures that exceeded Garfield's budget.

It is easy to call for the principal to achieve unity of purpose but quite another matter for him or her to achieve it. Nevertheless, effective urban principals do tackle this issue, knowing its difficulties and pitfalls full well.

Internally, Hagen followed a similar strategy. She bought off teachers who were potential critics by placing them on special assignment. Instead of having a six-class teaching load, these "pet" teachers were released from teaching altogether and given special jobs in the school—curriculum specialist, bilingual consultant, technology resource teacher, or school-to-work coordinator, for example. The children these teachers should have taught were added to the classes of other teachers, thus raising average class size in the school from 30 to 35. The morale of the entire faculty plummeted as most teachers became overburdened and Hagen's pets spent their days trying to appear busy.

Finally, a series of student shootings focused the media on the school for a sustained period and forced the superintendent to reassign Hagen to the central office. Miguel Hernandez, a successful assistant principal, was brought in to "turn the school around."

Hernandez speaks Spanish fluently, has lived in the community his entire life, and graduated from Garfield. He organized the community to change the name of the school to Cesar Chavez and set about building a new climate in the school. During his first year, Hernandez faced the animosity of parents whose jobs he sought to eliminate, community leaders who stood to lose control of the school council, and veteran teachers who had filed grievances with the teachers union because he tried to put them back in the classroom. In addition, most of the teachers he expected to support him had put in for transfers to other schools before he initiated these actions.

Analysis

Mr. Hernandez faces two very real issues. Who are his constituents in restructuring this nonfunctioning school? How should he galvanize them into action? Ms. Hagen was skillful at implementing three basic principles of leadership: unity of purpose, team building, and commitment to task. Unfortunately, her purposes were nefarious. She gained unity of purpose by channeling as much money out of this school budget and into parents' pockets and community agencies as possible. Second, Hagen was effective at team building. Local groups, newspapers, churches, and political groups were all built into effective teams that cooperated to keep the payoffs flowing. Finally, Hagen had her supporters so committed to these tasks that they persisted and continued to fight for their payola even after her departure. Though there is nothing wrong with paying parents for their participation on committees on a regular basis, the situation Hagen created clearly led to a misuse of school funds.

Hernandez must now use these same three principles to rebuild the school in ways that best serve the interests of the children. The principles of leadership do not change, but the purposes for their implementation will. Hernandez must begin by not trying to hide or cover up previous school mismanagement. It will be to his advantage to help people see how far down he has to start to rebuild this school community. His first constituency is the children. Next, he can get involved in new teacher selection rather than accept assignments from the central office. Hernandez can also find sincere, honest parents and community leaders who will work with the school in positive ways.

The principles of leadership do not change, but the purposes for their implementation will.

At the same time, the clock is ticking. In highly visible situations such as these, the honeymoon period for Hernandez will be one year—perhaps less. More-over, the lawsuits and teacher grievances he inherited will soon become his, and he will be expected to resolve them.

The common thread among these three principles of leadership is the message that Hernandez is not operating alone as the school savior. He must build coalitions, teams, support groups, and networks that will work in concert. In a situation this bad, people will perceive almost any honest initiative as a step forward. Statistical regression is likely to cause test scores this low to rise in response to any treatment. The danger Hernandez faces rests with this perception: He is accountable, because he is in charge. He needs all the help he can muster and organize among staff members, parents, and the community.

Discussion Questions

1. What are some specific steps Mr. Hernandez might take to create a new unity of purpose for this school?
2. What will lead previous wrongdoers to accept the fact that there will really be a new order in this school?
3. Is it necessary or unnecessary for the principal to maintain written records of the procedures he follows to rectify the previous mismanagement? Why?

Chapter 5

Schools Serving Children in Poverty

Star principals generate problems for themselves because they encourage people to think, and thinking inevitably leads to questioning school rules and practices.

For children in poverty, I believe that being successful in school is a matter of life and death. Their only hope of ever attaining a decent job—one that will pay for livable housing and sufficient health insurance—is to complete both high school and some level of postsecondary training. Students who drop out, run afoul of the criminal justice system, or become pregnant during their teen years are not likely ever to hold a job that will pay them a living wage. The difference between making it through high school or dropping out is frequently the difference between having a chance for a life with a future or becoming a no-hoper.

Extreme Views

One of the key predictors of principals who can be effective in poverty schools is the way they explain the large and growing number of students at risk of dropping out. At one extreme are those educators who blame the victim. This explanation fixes all the causes of the student's problems on his or her own inadequacies and on the inadequacies of his or her family and community. Given this perception, there is really nothing for which the school can be held accountable. If the student lacks basic language skills prior to kindergarten, has a dysfunctional family, or lives in a neighborhood characterized by gangs, drugs, violence, and crime, these are all matters beyond the aegis of the school. Schools do not cause these problems, nor are they organized to solve them.

Candidates for school principal frequently hold a "Don't look at us" view regarding the causes of youngsters being at risk. They also are likely to explain success in school on the basis of ability. It seems natural to these candidates that youngsters who are apparently brighter will do better than those who may have less genetic endowment.

This pattern of beliefs is an extreme liability, because it portends failure for those who hold it. Blaming the victim, his or her family, and the community for lack of school success—and attributing school success to innate ability—predisposes the holders of these views to rationalize their inaction and lack of accountability. Those who hold such beliefs ask, "What can you expect the school (or me) to do about all the debilitating conditions of urban poverty? What can the schools do with children who have less ability?" They explain the problems facing students at risk of failure by citing factors outside the aegis of the school. Their reasoning is that, if the causes of at-risk students exist in conditions outside of school, then the solutions must exist outside of school as well.

At the other extreme are educators equally aware of all the negative effects of poverty in urban life. These individuals, however, also identify problems caused by schools—for example, poor teachers, inadequate curriculum, overcrowded class-rooms, or inadequate materials and equipment—that might place youngsters at risk of failing or dropping out. Where do children lose their basic curiosity in learning? In which institution do children fail to learn basic skills? Where do girls learn they are not good in science and math? Educators who understand that schools contrib-ute to creating at-risk youngsters are willing to accept responsibility and hold schools accountable for solving the problem. Such individuals have a different explanation for success in school, attributing it to effort rather than ability. This perspective leads them to believe that schools and educators can be held account-able for generating effort. By defining a significant portion of the cause for being at risk to in-school conditions, these individuals believe solutions are also within the purview of the school and its teachers.

Assuming Accountability

The principals needed in urban schools serving a majority of at-risk students must believe in students' potential. They must model the philosophy that generating effort can make them successful. They must maintain that the school has the power to engage students in meaningful learning regardless—or in spite of—living condi-tions. This task will not be simple. Burned out teachers, and even some adequate ones, typically blame the victims for learning deficiencies rather than themselves. This shift of blame is a natural coping device. Indeed, if teachers have children failing to learn, there are only two options: either something is wrong with the students, or something is wrong with the teacher and his or her methods. Teachers who attribute all the blame to students, their families, and backgrounds may be struggling with their own self-concepts. They may be unable to face the reality that they are performing inadequately and must change. They typically create support groups and encourage each other by saying, "They expect us to do everything for these children when there is nothing more we can do."

The essential job of the principal in implementing a belief in students' potential is to move teachers from blaming the victim to assuming accountability for what and how much children can learn. For the principal to accomplish this incredibly difficult task, he or she must personally believe in students' potential. If the principal believes effort rather than genetic endowment is the best explanation of success in school, then he or she may be able to change resistant teachers. However, if the principal believes in the ability paradigm and that the forces of poverty cannot be overcome by improving schools, then he or she becomes the spokesperson and leader of faculty burn-outs.

In short, the assumption of accountability is based on the conviction that improving schools is possible and will make a difference in the educational achievement of youngsters in poverty. Without this conviction, there can be no school accountability; there will be only whining about the impossible job of working with students in poverty. No reasonable person expects schools to solve problems of abuse, unemployment, violence, drugs, gangs, racism, poor housing, and inadequate health care. Reasonable people can point to specific schools serving children in poverty in which children are learning at two and three times the rate of similar children in similar schools in similar neighborhoods. Why are some schools doing so much better than other schools in the same districts? An important part of the explanation lies in the ideology of the principal. The principal who accepts responsibility for students' learning may lead the staff to equally accountable behavior.

Case 4: Home Visits

Janet Hawkins is in her fifth year as principal of Lincoln Elementary School. She has carefully developed a parent-friendly school. Parents are involved in all facets of the school program.

Hawkins's educational philosophy is that children at risk of falling behind in school and dropping out face many debilitating life conditions: poverty, poor health care, inadequate housing, family crises, abuse, gangs, violence, or unemployed caregivers. She also knows other reasons children in her school are not achieving as well as they might. For example, the school has several teachers of primary grades who are less than satisfactory. In addition, the school has an inadequate supply of trade books, art supplies, paper, and science equipment. Moreover, until the new law limiting class size in the primary grades took effect, almost all classes had more than 30 students. Grades four and five still exceed 30 students per classroom. Finally, the curriculum of the district is not aligned with achievement tests. Children who seem to be working at grade level score below grade level on such tests. Hawkins is aware of both home and school conditions causing her children to be at high risk of school failure.

Hawkins's commitment to parental involvement is starting to bear positive results for the school. While some parents remain unreachable and others abuse their children, her persistent efforts have involved more parents in school activities each year. With the help of the school system's central office research department, Hawkins can show that, in the classrooms where teachers and parents have close and supportive relationships, children's behavior has improved. Test score averages are also higher in these classrooms compared with others in the building.

Hawkins uses school funds to pay for teachers to attend workshops on parental relations. She has also installed telephones in every classroom, allowing teachers to make outside calls.

The teachers who have adopted Hawkins's philosophy now engage in several behaviors on a regular basis. They call children's homes and frequently report children's positive accomplishments during the school day. These teachers all make home visits. For the few cases in which parents prefer not to have a teacher visit their homes, meetings are arranged in shopping malls and local restaurants. Children are frequently involved in these conferences. In fact, students now expect their teachers and parents to know each other well and communicate frequently. This level of cooperation is making a real difference in the lives and accomplish-

The essential job of the principal in implementing a belief in students' potential is to move teachers from blaming the victim to assuming accountability for what and how much children can learn. For the principal to accomplish this incredibly difficult task, he or she must personally believe in students' potential.

Chapter 5

ments of children at Lincoln Elementary School.

Several veteran teachers have developed a clear resistance to making home visits. These teachers simply reject the notion that meeting parents anywhere off school grounds is part of their job. They raise issues of safety and reject even meeting on neutral ground. These teachers claim they are too busy teaching to be calling homes with positive reports during the school day. They cite parents who are drug addicts and child abusers to show why their efforts would be wasted.

Significantly, 90 percent of the Lincoln students' parents are members of minority culture groups—though most of the veteran teachers who resist the home-visit strategy are European Americans. Some European Americans are among the teacher group participating in home visitations, but the majority of these teachers are members of minority groups: African Americans, Hispanics, and Hmong. While this ethnic division among teachers is not discussed openly, Hawkins, the teachers, and the parents are all aware of it. Hawkins is starting to wonder if the children are also aware of it.

The entire issue has been brought to a head by a positive newspaper story featuring the home visits of effective Lincoln teachers. Hawkins and a majority of her teachers have instituted a home-visitation policy for student teachers. A nearby university has been informed that student teachers unwilling to join cooperating teachers on visits with parents in their homes and at other off-school sites will not be welcome at Lincoln School. Hawkins has also informed the university's dean that class conflicts in students' schedules would not be an acceptable excuse. "If we're training teachers to teach in the real world," Hawkins reasoned, "they need to see what the total job of successful teachers of children in poverty really involves." This statement represents the view of most Lincoln faculty members.

The disgruntled veteran teachers have filed a grievance with the teachers' union. The contract states their hours of work and does not require them to make home visits with parents or caregivers. Several of the resisting teachers' spouses are well-to-do professionals and business people, including two who are lawyers. Hawkins has learned about meetings between some of her veteran teachers and these attorneys to explore the possibility of charging her with harassment in the workplace.

Hawkins has decided that the best way to handle this situation is to ease the pressure she has been putting on teachers. She has informally made it known that teachers committed to home visits will continue to be facilitated in their efforts and teachers not making home visits will be scheduled to have conferences with parents in the school building. This dual policy has been in effect for the first half of the school year. Yet it does not seem to have assuaged the veteran teachers. In fact, they seem more disgruntled than ever. Hawkins is anticipating a serious blowup at any time.

Analysis

Whenever some teachers show up other teachers as being less committed, there will be strong resentment. At this point in the development of the Lincoln Elementary School problem, it will be difficult for Ms. Hawkins to defuse the issue. The veteran teachers correctly see her ideology and behavior as the basic cause of the problem. The fact that Hawkins's ideology is a sound one makes the situation worse for the dissenters. Short of renouncing her belief system, these teachers have no reason to trust or be mollified by her.

Whenever some teachers show up other teachers as being less committed, there will be strong resentment. At this point it will be difficult to defuse the issue.

If the disgruntled teachers are sufficient in number to form a support group among themselves, this issue may not be resolvable except by some legal rulings. Participants may modify the union contract to permit both sets of teacher practices to coexist. There may need to be formal arbitration to determine if the veteran teachers are indeed being harassed.

Hawkins is discovering that simply being right and doing good things does not prevent trouble. Indeed, doing the best thing for children will often cause more work and stress for the star principal. Still, Hawkins should have anticipated the reaction of the veteran teachers. Unless she had a concomitant plan for their early retirements or transfers, Hawkins should have known they planned to continue teaching at Lincoln. Indeed, she should have expected these teachers to organize themselves into more effective resisters and blockers. Hawkins could have made home visits voluntary from the outset. However, this strategy may not have worked, because it would have become obvious that teachers making home visits were getting better results and greater recognition from parents, children, and the principal.

The best course for Hawkins to follow would have been simple honesty.

Chapter 5

Anticipating resistance, she should have explored legalities and the union contract from the outset—not because it would have deterred her from implementing a policy of home visits but because she would have known what to expect and how to plan countermeasures at every step. Hawkins must persist in doing what is best for the children *and* work on all the bureaucratic barriers that inevitably arise in opposition to doing the right thing. She now must stick to her convictions on the home-visitation policy and work through the legal and contractual issues. Anticipating these roadblocks would not have prevented this problem, but it would have decreased stress and personal animosities. Everyone would have known her intentions, and Hawkins could have secured allies among her superiors. As the situation stands now, she can only play "catch up" and "damage control."

Discussion Questions

1. What is the best possible outcome Ms. Hawkins can still achieve in this situation?
2. If Hawkins could start over, knowing what she now knows, what policy would be best regarding home visits?
3. What role, if any, do parents have in the resolution of this problem?

Chapter 6

Accountable Instructional Leadership

To be the "instructional leader" does not require that a principal be the best teacher or know the most about curriculum. It requires making sure the school spends its resources in a manner that reflects the school's priorities.

Much of the inordinate stress for principals of schools serving children in poverty stems from being accountable for staff members whose actions they can affect but not control. For this reason, star principals focus their energy on improving the conditions under which teachers and staff work. By enabling good things to happen and removing obstacles to reach school goals, these principals exert stronger impact on staff behavior than if they tried influencing individuals directly or simply ordered compliance. For example, reducing class sizes or providing teacher aides has a greater influence on changing instructional methods than observing classes or holding individual conferences with teachers.

Another source of the principal's stress is that he or she has even less control over superiors. The superintendent and central office send downward a steady flow of budget changes, regulations, paperwork, school board policies, and new initiatives. The weak, ineffective principal passes all or most of this chaos down to the staff. The star principal serves as a buffer between the increasing demands of the system and the work of teachers. This absorption of upward stress from ineffective staff members, along with the simultaneous absorption of downward stress from central office demands, lowers principals' morale and causes burnout.

How a principal handles this double whammy depends upon his or her problem-solving ability. This ability requires a mixture of thinking creatively and learning from experience. While these attributes contribute to the principal's ability to function as a problem solver, the essential element really has more to do with persistence. Few if any problems of importance can be solved by a one-time treatment. Almost every conflict a principal addresses must be faced over and over—not because the treatment is wrong but because it must be applied consistently over time to have any effect. Implementing new programs, making changes in scheduling, improving computer use, and building business partnerships all involve solving problems over extended periods. Human problems require even greater persistence. However, regardless of the conditions they face—implementing a new method of instruction, improving parental involvement, or solving some interpersonal conflict among staff members—star principals never flag. They are committed to the struggle required to improve their schools. The ultimate example is their persistence in getting rid of ineffective staff, regardless of hoops to be jumped, paper work, legalities, or difficult human relations.

Persistence

The personal attribute most predictive of a principal's future behavior is his or her proclivity to persist in meeting the stated goals of the school. Indeed, this attribute predicts success in any field. It is effort rather than ability that accounts for most people's success. A quotation attributed to Calvin Coolidge stated it this way:

> Nothing in the world can take the place of persistence. Talent will not: nothing is more common than unsuccessful men with talent. Genius will not: unrewarded genius is almost a proverb. Education will not: the world is full of educated derelicts. Persistence and determination alone are omnipotent.

To function as the genuine instructional leader of the school and not its business manager, the principal must demonstrate certain attributes. Foremost is the willingness to be accountable. The principal who says, "The university prepared these teachers and the Human Resources Department hired them, so what do you want from me?" does not understand the accountability model under which he or she is operating. Neither does the more experienced principal who says, "It may take up to $200,000 to get rid of this teacher. If we do spend the time and energy and are successful, then central office will probably deduct these costs from my school budget." No rationalization can overcome the need for the principal to work persistently at getting poor teachers out of the school.

By never giving up and by continuing to apply specific treatments, improvement is more likely to occur than by giving in or by trying to live with a problem. In the case of ineffective teachers who are damaging children's life opportunities, the principal should become a source of stress rather than the individual who absorbs it. Some teachers will seek to remove themselves from a school if the principal persists with a regular schedule of observations, evaluations of plans, and conferences in which new objectives and deadlines for performance are established. There are no one-time solutions to this problem. It takes consistent effort over time.

Selecting New Teachers

Star principals know the effort and costs required to remove weak teachers, or even to improve some of their teaching methods. Consequently, they spend much time and energy on selecting new teachers. Though cities typically follow a system in which the initial screening of teachers is conducted by the central office, individual schools usually have the final voice in accepting applicants. In most cases, the principal has the major voice in accepting a particular teacher for the building. In some cities, a parent/community board may make the final determination. The problem of shortage comes into play in this initial assignment process. In districts scrambling for teachers, it is common to hire large numbers of individuals on temporary or provisional licenses. Frequently, such long-term substitutes are simply doled out from the central office to cover vacancies. The school principal still must have the major voice in accepting these appointees, because many of them will function as regular teachers in the building for a full year or longer. It is a flawed system that gives a principal voice in determining regularly assigned teachers but none in selecting substitutes simply because they carry a provisional label. The principal must actively seek to be accountable for all the teachers assigned to the building, regardless of their license designations.

To interview new teacher candidates, principals may want to refer to the method presented in *Star Teachers of Children in Poverty* (Haberman 1995). Simply asking his or her favorite questions may lead a principal to select teachers who can verbalize clichés—yet such a practice likely will not predict which candidates will be able to teach children in poverty. If the central office of the district already uses this or another validated interview to screen candidates, the principal should still become familiar with its contents and procedures. In-service training, as with any other teacher education, only makes a difference if the teachers selected initially are predisposed to accept and implement that training. Without careful selection, traditional forms of preservice and in-service staff development are irrelevant to the practice of teachers serving children in poverty.

To function as the instructional leader, the principal must know and keep current with the most effective methods of instruction for generating results with students. He or she must be an expert consumer of these instructional strategies in order to answer two questions: How can teachers learn, practice, and improve effective strategies? What conditions can he or she provide to facilitate implementing these activities?

Case 5: Dance of the Lemons

Jake Nelson is concluding his second year as principal of Madison High School. He was hired to "turn the school around," and during his first year brought the building under control and made it a safe haven for students and staff members. Located adjacent to a housing project notorious for drugs, gangs, and violence, Nelson had a remarkable first year. He worked with police, parents, the community, the housing authority, and even some gang leaders to create a truce around Madison and its students. After all the evenings and weekends, he was exhausted; but the creation of a safe school environment is now a fact.

During his second year, Nelson directed his primary attention to functioning as an instructional leader. He knows that no school can be better than its teachers. As principal, he has devoted significant hours to identifying a few star teachers, many satisfactory teachers, and several weak teachers in need of improvement. He has also tried to improve working conditions.

Examining the employment backgrounds of his weak teachers, Nelson learned that they all transferred from other schools with thick folders indicating that numerous supervisors, mentors, and resource teachers had devoted much time and energy trying to help them. These weak teachers all have eight or more years of teaching experience and hold master's degrees. The practice in the district is to permit teachers with seniority to transfer first—a practice dubbed the "dance of the lemons."

Nelson identified seven weak teachers but decided he could not work with all of them at once. During the second year of his administration, he decided to zero in on the weakest teacher and see what could be done. If he could remove this extreme case from the school, Nelson would be sending a signal that weak teachers who waste students' time will no longer be transferred but dismissed.

After consulting with his assistants and the department chair, Nelson chose Adelaide Johnson as his first effort at instructional improvement. Johnson is a mathematics teacher who drives students out of her classes. By mid-semester, one-half of the students in her classes typically fail to show up; by semester's end, she is usually down to one-third of the initial enrollment. Students who drop out of Madison High School frequently cite her among their reasons for leaving. Johnson files the most referrals to Madison's office for discipline and suspension and comes in first with complaints from parents. These complaints involve the manner in which the math teacher treats, grades, or communicates with students.

Johnson's achievement scores are typically the lowest of all the math teachers. Regardless of how few of her students take the required final examinations for graduation, her classes consistently score the lowest.

Observations of Johnson by department chairs and central office supervisors are consistently poor. She never motivates or encourages her students; she never prompts questions and seldom checks homework. Students in her classes are frequently off task, sleeping, or doing other schoolwork. Johnson's method is to proceed through textbooks, assigning pages in sequence. She seems oblivious that students are not following along with her and act completely uninvolved. There are frequent "discipline problems" as students busy themselves with each other, attempting somehow to fill up the "math" hour.

Johnson attributes her students' lack of learning to (1) previous teachers who did not "teach these kids the basics," (2) poor home conditions in which "parents do not supervise homework," and (3) a basic lack of "ability and math intelligence." Yet she prepares no materials. Her plan book only lists the page number in the text she is covering. Use of computers is never more than a skill-and-drill program.

Johnson uses all her sick days, which means she is absent due to illness 1 out of every 10 days. She has all the doctors' notes required to support these absences. Johnson also leaves during many days when she becomes ill at school but has been in attendance a sufficient number of hours to be considered present according to the school contract. She also uses all special days and professional days allowed by the teacher contract. Thus, an examination of her attendance record reveals that Johnson typically teaches approximately 150 days of the 181-day school year.

Furthermore, Johnson arrives precisely 15 minutes prior to school and leaves precisely 15 minutes after school, as allowed by the contract. She participates in no committees, engages in no out-of-class activities, and attends no meetings of any kind. When she reached the top of the salary schedule by taking a mail-order

All principals must become experts at the specifics of dismissal procedures. Whatever the difficulty involved, the effort to remove weak teachers must be pursued.

master's degree, she ceased her "in-service development."

In conferencing with Johnson in early fall, Nelson noted that she remained silent. The principal indicated he was initiating step one of the dismissal process, which requires notification of cause, dates for making observations of teaching, and the completion of lengthy written forms. After one week, Nelson received notification that Johnson had filed a union grievance against him on two counts: discrimination (only European Americans were to observe her teaching, and Johnson is African American) and harassment (Nelson has not initiated dismissal procedures against European-American teachers doing the same things Johnson is accused of doing).

Nelson has persisted through all the complex procedures for dismissal and is preparing a defense against the union grievance. He is now spending at least ten hours per week on this case in addition to a great deal of emotional energy.

After the winter break, Nelson is informed that Johnson has reported experiencing an emotional breakdown from the stress. She has checked herself into a hospital and engaged a lawyer to sue the district for medical expenses plus $1 million in damages. With this medical validation, Johnson maintains she is also covered by the federal law protecting the disabled. The union is supporting her case.

The lawyer for the school system has informed Nelson that the district has decided to settle with Johnson rather than take the case to court. The counsel points to several steps with which Nelson or his staff did not comply in the time periods specifically required by the union contract. Several forms were also not completed with sufficient copies. The superintendent informs Nelson that he will "support" him. What this "support" means is that, when a settlement is reached with Johnson, only half of the money will be taken out of the Madison High School budget. After negotiations, which Nelson has to keep confidential, the system settles with Johnson for $500,000. She is also allowed to return to another high school in the district after one year's paid leave. Nelson decides to accept the "reality" that, although he has several other weak teachers, he will have to learn to live with them. He cannot go through this nightmare again.

Analysis

All principals must become experts at the specifics of dismissal procedures. The fact that these procedures are extremely complex, take up a great deal of time, and consume much emotional energy is no excuse. Whatever the difficulty involved, the effort to remove weak teachers must be pursued.

In this case, the principal was naive. Mr. Nelson should have been thoroughly versed in all the required steps and procedures for teacher removal before he began the process. He should have anticipated possible options that Ms. Johnson might take and prepared himself for them. This preparation should include meeting with and learning from the school system's lawyers, as well as meeting with and learning from other principals in the district who have pursued dismissal actions with successful conclusions. Nelson should have familiarized himself with the protections offered in the teacher contract to those who claim medical disabilities. He should also understand that it is not uncommon for inadequate teachers to demonstrate remarkable ability at protecting their self-interests. When people's financial survival is at stake, they should not be expected to leave quietly. Finally, charges of harassment and discrimination are also quite common in these cases. Nelson should have familiarized himself thoroughly with the law. Though an African American himself, Nelson should have made certain that those observing Johnson's teaching included some African Americans. He might have simultaneously instituted dismissal procedures against another weak European-American teacher so that a charge of discrimination on the basis of race or ethnicity could not be alleged.

Getting rid of poor teachers is a must for the effective principal. So too is the need to do the homework and learn the precise provisions of the union contract, as well as state and federal laws regarding employees' workplace rights. The principal who does not persist and allows burnouts to beat him or her by using the complexities of law and contracts is only hurting the children he or she is supposed to be protecting. If the procedures for dismissal are too difficult for the principal to learn and implement, he or she cannot function in the role of principal.

Discussion Questions

1. On which issues is the teacher, Ms. Johnson, correct?
2. Discuss Mr. Nelson's initial decision that "he could not work with" the seven weak teachers at once.
3. If you were Nelson's superior, what three points would you want him to understand?

Chapter 7

Creating a Positive School Climate and Fighting Burnout

Urban school bureaucracy is not benign. It sets up serious obstacles to teaching and learning. The star principal is on a constant vigil to mitigate the impact of this intrusive chaos.

Violence is rarely absent and seldom late from schools serving children in poverty. Every day it accompanies students, teachers, principals, and everyone else into the buildings. Youngsters' real-world concerns also come to schools via the media and other impacting influences; they seep through the cracks of school buildings like pollution and through students like a virus. How schools react to violence among youth in poverty determines whether schools empower students with new options or leave them feeling stripped bare (Dill 1999). Central to this decision is the school principal.

Schools alone cannot change a violent society, but they can (1) stop making the problems worse, (2) teach alternatives to violence, (3) get more youngsters to care about the consequences of their behavior, and (4) improve the quality of learning. The goal of making the school a safe haven in which youngsters might gain some respite from violence to think and learn is a good one. Yet it cannot be realized apart from improving what and how teachers teach, examining how principals administer school rules, and creating an antiviolent vision shared by everyone in the building.

The argument that making schools safe havens is not likely to stamp out violence in the total society should not deter us from the effort. Saving more youngsters from lives of nonparticipation and desperation is a sufficiently worthwhile goal to pursue. Making present forms of schooling less violent cannot await the restructuring of schools promised by various change agents. Much can—and must—be done immediately; effective changes will involve more than a university course or in-service workshop in violence prevention.

A Survey of Students

A sample group of middle school students in Milwaukee, Wisconsin, ages 13–15, was asked its views on violence (Haberman and Dill 1995), as shown in figure 1 below. This cohort consisted of 60 African Americans, 1 Hispanic, and 4 European Americans.

Figure 1

Middle School Students' Views on School Violence	Yes	No	Don't Know
1. If there's an argument, kids should just settle it after school among themselves.	43	7	14
2. If there's an argument, the principal should be warned and stop the fight.	19	35	11
3. If everyone could bring a knife or gun to school, students would feel safer.	23	41	1
4. Students and teachers together can cut down on the fear in school.	29	12	21
5. Students who fight in school should be punished by teachers and principals.	6	42	10
6. Students should have more say-so in how arguments are settled.	38	6	14

Note: Only items 2 and 3 account for all 65 respondents.
In answer to the other items, some students made no response.

Reprinted from M. Haberman and V. S. Dill. 1995. Commitment to violence among teenagers in poverty. *Kappa Delta Pi Record* 31(4): 150.

The teacher of the students surveyed discussed their responses with them. He reported that the students connected items 1, 2, and 6 in their thinking. In effect, the respondents believed students should have more say-so in settling arguments (item 6), because the best thing to do is step outside and fight it out (item 1) and not squeal to any authority (item 2). The students saw these items as different from item 5, which referred to fights *in* school. Location apparently seemed to matter: out-of-school violence was okay; in-school was not. None of these students suggested any alternative to violence as a means of settling disputes.

As the teacher discussed the students' beliefs about violence with them, they seemed to connect items 3 and 4. Most students—those responding "No" and "Don't Know"—did not know if anything could be done to cut down on school violence. The majority believed that informing the principal (or another authority figure) would not solve the problem.

Respondents indicated that violence is a fact of everyday life and something they have to face alone or with trusted allies (for example, gangs, peers, or family members). Preventing violence was never discussed in terms of seeking out any duly constituted authorities, such as school personnel or police officers. Students rejected reporting violence to authorities for two reasons: They believe it shows that one is a coward or is in some way incapable of taking care of himself or herself, and that "authority" is never around when you need it.

In follow-up discussions, other values were expressed that students seemed to accept without dissent. Among these were the following: European Americans do not know how to fight or take care of themselves. Fighting is natural and to be expected. Every life situation involves a boss or top dog and others who do what they are told.

The Milwaukee teenagers were also asked, "When is it okay to hit someone?" and "When is it okay to kill someone?" Amazingly, their responses were the same to both questions:

★ "When they talk crazy."
★ "When you are provoked."
★ "When you think they're bossy."
★ "When they say something smart."

Only one youth stated, "It's not okay to hit or kill anyone." No other member of the cohort responded to this idea or seemed to take note of it in any way.

Counteracting School Violence

Administrators and principals of schools serving children in poverty should internalize the following list of principles. In fact, a star principal will model these beliefs and establish an expectation among staff members that they too should live by them.

1. Whatever is illegal outside of school cannot be treated as if it were not a crime inside of school. Making the school a safe haven for youngsters who live in violent communities does not mean creating a medieval sanctuary civil authorities may not enter. If a student sets a fire or carries a weapon, it is not within the purview of the principal to decide that "no one was really hurt," or that "the school program was not impeded in any way." Crimes do not transform into something else because they are perpetrated in schools.

2. The processes of school management and discipline are more important than the outcomes. The manner in which particular disciplinary cases are handled teaches students more than detentions or suspensions. Students must not have their belief that power is everything reinforced. Principals and teachers must demonstrate repeatedly that thinking, reasoning, and working through problems are respectable alternatives to violence. Dispensing school justice en masse on the basis of inflexible rules, rather than on an individual basis, reinforces students' sense of isolation and victimization: "How much suspension did you get? Two days? A week?" Students must be freed from seeing everyone as either a perpetrator or a victim. This shift can only be accomplished when school processes involve taking time to communicate thoroughly, involve all participants, and demonstrate an in-depth concern for youngsters, teachers, and staff. If school officials *begin* by assuming they do not have enough time or person power to administer individualized, careful processes, they are, in effect, conceding they cannot decrease the violence. Indeed, we can be certain that a system of only enforcement and control, impersonally administered and emphasizing punishment, will make matters worse. It will play into the limited worldview most youth in poverty embrace: Power is everything. They believe it is the school's responsibility to *make them* behave, just as it is the school's responsibility to *make them* learn.

3. Problems of violence are not intrusions on the school program; they are an integral part of it. Teaching students to care about and predict the consequences of their behavior must be part of the school program. Options to violence—such as peer mediation or conflict resolution—must be actively modeled every day in every class. Subject-matter "fights," for example, can serve a useful purpose. Youngsters can be taught to deal legitimately and passionately with rival explanations and alternative solutions to problems in various subject matters. Forms of communication for resolving conflicts are not behaviors students of poverty bring to school automatically, somehow know naturally, or think up on their own. Every curricular subject in schools serving youth in poverty can emphasize consistently how reasonable people resolve conflicts.

Education is *living* rather than *preparation* for living. Students must deal with real problems now to learn what they must know for later in life. They can be protected from some of the violence they face in their communities when they attend school. Principals of schools engulfed in a climate of violence must make its elimination on school grounds a priority. Schools cannot, of course, solve society's violence problem on their own. Principals, however, should not be deterred from fostering gentle teaching and acts of de-escalation to avoid making matters worse (Haberman 1994).

Case 6: Fires

Ben Abraham has been principal of Lakeview Elementary School for 25 years. He has become a community institution in the churches and with business leaders. Politicians, the police, and long-time residents all know and respect him. In deference to him, the Great Cities School District has let his school remain K–8 rather than send the top three grades to various middle schools.

Abraham is planning to retire. Because he loves the school and wants to perpetuate what he has created for the children, the principal has been grooming a successor. Enrique Fernandez is a fine assistant principal. He is hard working and devoted to the students, their families, and the community.

Although their styles differ, both individuals are extremely committed professionals. Abraham appears laid back and outwardly calm. Experience has taught him that there will always be tomorrow and that he must never burn bridges with people today—especially those with whom he must work. Fernandez is more of a here-and-now dynamo; every issue seems to be an emergency to solve completely right away. Abraham has high hopes for Fernandez, already teaching him ways to defuse and de-escalate problems. Together, over the past year and a half, they have made remarkable improvements in Lakeview's school achievement, climate, and parental relations.

Of particular pride to Abraham is the school climate. Even casual visitors make supportive comments: "This is a very special place." "What a friendly atmosphere." "The teachers and students all seem to be on the same page." Abraham believes his secret has been the creation of a school family. If a youngster has medical, clothing, home-environment, or personal needs, there always seems to be someone at Lakeview ready to help. Behind them all is Abraham.

In the past few years, gang activity in the community has escalated. The movement of Hispanics and Asian Americans into an area formerly comprised solely of African Americans seems to have caused "turf wars." Despite Lakeview's many advances, in the past year, graffiti has increased all over school grounds. "Taggers" are now spraying within the school. Gang-related clothing and emblems have become apparent. Disputes from outside the school are being brought into the building, involving both males and females. Competition for new gang members has moved down from seventh and eighth grades; some sixth graders are now becoming involved. The once-tranquil climate of Lakeview is being adversely affected. Teachers report more fights for no apparent reason and more clothing destroyed or stolen.

Abraham has been very sensitive to the negative impact of turf battles and competition for new members. He has been meeting with parent groups every evening. On weekends, he visits churches and homes. He has initiated several projects with school and state funds to counteract gangs. Abraham and Fernandez meet almost daily with police officials and social workers. Working on this problem has left Abraham exhausted. Nevertheless, he believes he is saving his school and wants to maintain it as a safe haven for his students. Abraham remains convinced that he can keep the school an island of hope in a sea of trouble.

Setting fires is a serious crime, and wrongdoers must be punished. Whatever is illegal in the larger society is also illegal in a school building.

In September, the year began as usual, except that there seemed to be more fire drills. The faculty and then the students realized that these alarms were more than just planned drills. By October, they increased to one per week; by November, two per week. Sometimes an alarm lever was pulled. At other times, however, a fire was actually started in a trash can or locker. By December, it became clear that someone was also setting off alarms by spray cans aimed at smoke detectors.

Fernandez established early in the year that these alarms were the activities of "wanna-bes" pledging to become gang members. The fire department was deeply concerned, because they simply did not have the manpower to respond. The police with whom the administrators conferred expressed helplessness at controlling events on school grounds.

Abraham increased the number of safety aides. He also recruited a corps of parent volunteers to patrol school grounds on evenings and weekends. Using portable telephones, these groups were able to call—usually late at night—and report fires being set. Abraham or Fernandez would then immediately call the police. Unfortunately, even this quick action did not stop the activity. Most debilitating were alarms set off during the school day. As the weather grew severe, it was an increasing hardship to keep emptying the building.

At this point, the activities of the two administrators diverged somewhat. Fernandez talked to individuals who might serve as witnesses. He pursued the perpetrators and worked closely with the police. Abraham sought out individuals who might help resolve the problem. He called a half-day school assembly and invited parents and community representatives. There were small-group sessions for brainstorming about what might be done. At one extreme were suggestions for imprisoning the "arsonists." At the other extreme was the suggestion that Abraham have a private meeting with gang leaders and agree to their aegis over certain turf—for example, one gang would have the north playground, another the west playground, and a third the streets south and east of the building. The consensus of the assembly was that all students, teachers, and staff had a responsibility to join hands and work to prevent and stamp out this activity.

Analysis

Mr. Fernandez was correct in pursuing the legal aspect of this problem. Setting fires is a serious crime, and wrongdoers must be punished. Whatever is illegal in the larger society is also illegal in a school building. Arson is a crime everywhere. Yet Fernandez could not solve this problem working entirely through legal channels.

Mr. Abraham showed good judgment by involving the whole school community. It is the school climate that is at stake in such situations, and all stakeholders must be involved. It is also an important process to allow students, faculty, and staff members a voice in what to do. All constituencies must feel that this is "our" building and that "we" must protect it. In truth, it would take everyone working together to stop these fires.

Administrators must listen to the extremely punitive suggestions that come out of such assemblies. Arson is a crime, and administrators must be prepared to regard it as such. Obviously, however, the criminal justice system by itself will not resolve this type of problem. More than arrests must be contemplated. Escalating the threat of arrest was a necessary but insufficient response to this problem, because most of the perpetrators were not being caught. As the danger of possible arrest increased, gangs would become more motivated to use this activity as a test of prospective members' courage.

Abraham should have rejected outright any suggestion that he would meet with gang leaders and legitimize their control over various physical spaces. Such an action would not be a truce but a capitulation on his part. Law and order must be upheld throughout the building and on all school property. Abraham has the job of upholding the position that the setting of fires is a crime that will lead to expulsion and arrest.

Coming out of Abraham's school assembly was the heightened sensitivity of the total school community around several key concepts: "This is *our* school; we have to take care of it." "The few doing this are hurting all of *us*—wasting our time and controlling us." It was especially gratifying to Abraham that most of the sixth-, seventh-, and eighth-grade teachers are incorporating this real-life problem into their classroom teaching: "When you tell on someone setting a fire, is it 'ratting' or are you protecting people's lives?" "If you have information to give, is there some way to give it anonymously, or do you have to risk being hurt?" Together, teachers and students have tried to answer these questions and create a system in which seeking to prevent fires would become a shared responsibility and not just Abraham's job. In the process of grappling with this issue, the school actually drew closer in the face of more fire alarms. By involving teachers and students in problem-solving ways of cutting down on fires, Abraham made the school curriculum actual practice in living rather than preparation for later life.

In the long term, the best hope of these administrators is to keep this fire issue on the "front burner" and not let it be forgotten, even as the number of false alarms begins to decrease. Keeping everyone watchful and alert and in communication about fire safety will enhance the togetherness felt in the school community. It is unfortunate that children in urban poverty must deal with such an issue, but this is the reality of life in modern society. There is no way to keep the problems of the larger society out of the school. Instead, capable administrators can work toward making their schools safe havens. To do so, however, they must secure and coordinate the support of everyone involved.

Discussion Questions

1. What would be different about this problem if it occurred in a senior high school?

2. What can Mr. Abraham do in this case to counteract the belief that students who report wrongdoers are "rats?"
3. What human resources might Abraham coordinate and bring to bear on this issue?

Chapter 8

Evaluation

Teachers will forgive almost any criticism provided it is wrong. They will never forgive or forget a criticism that is accurate.

The inadequate principal rarely considers his or her own evaluation. If he or she has not crossed the superintendent, been cited by the school board, or incurred the ire of important central-office administrators, then this type of principal assumes that nothing has changed. The tacit criteria this nonproducer uses combine "don't cause waves" and "stay in the background." He or she has no proactive objectives. Such an individual is likely to perform the minimum maintenance functions required for the management of the school, including all the necessary paperwork and reports for the central office. In short, the nonproducer believes the administrator's job is to avoid causing trouble.

The principal who operates in this way likely will seek teachers and staff members who quietly comply and do nothing more. Teachers who want to do things differently to help students learn more will receive little support from such a principal. Staff members in such a school can readily predict the principal's reaction to just about any new initiative. If it will make the principal look good and not threaten any individual or group with the power to hurt him or her, then the principal will likely be in favor of it. If there is any risk that an individual or group whose approval he or she covets may criticize the principal for pursuing the initiative, then he or she will say, "Forget it."

Every urban district has its share of these job-holder principals. The problem is that many districts continue to hire more of them rather than initiate better means of selection. One reason a new urban superintendent's job is so challenging stems from inheriting a substantial cadre of these administrative non-leaders. Outwardly, these principals appear to conform to the initiatives of the new superintendent but, because they lack genuine leadership skills, they are unable to implement important goals and objectives. Many of these individuals are highly skilled at appearing to accomplish "things" even as a school regresses. Upon examination, however, there is a lot less going on in the school than meets the eye.

Evaluative Criteria

When star principals think of evaluation, they think of themselves first. They are willing to apply very difficult evaluative criteria to themselves, because they have a professional commitment to the children and the school. Such principals ask:

1. What criteria should be used to evaluate me?
2. Is achievement going up?
3. Is the school becoming a safer place more conducive to learning and work?
4. Are acts of violence, suspensions, and expulsions decreasing?
5. Are teachers seeking to transfer into the school?
6. Are parents trying to enroll their children?
7. How well are the graduates doing at the next school level or in the world of work?
8. How effectively are the school's resources being used?
9. Are the school's computers and laboratories utilized as fully as possible?
10. Is the school curriculum aligned with the measures used to assess learning?
11. Are the latest and best instructional strategies being used?
12. Are parents and caregivers involved in the life of the school?
13. Are children and families in need of social and human services being connected with those services?
14. Are the conditions of work that teachers believe would help children learn more being addressed?
15. Is there a way to give teachers the tools and materials they need, or are teachers spending their own money?
16. Are the bonds between teachers and caregivers being strengthened by home visits and other contacts outside the building?
17. Does every teacher have a telephone for making outside calls in the classroom?
18. What provisions are made for teachers to pursue their own teacher-development plans?
19. What provisions will help teachers defray the costs of their development plans?
20. What procedures, projects, or programs are in place to teach students alternatives to violence in solving problems?

21. Are teacher teams or groupings working as effectively as they might be?
22. Are the school's business partners visible and active in the life of the school?
23. Is the school's inclusion program working?
24. Are teacher grievances being filed by burned out teachers or by star teachers?
25. Are the business-management functions of the school being performed at an efficient level?
26. Do all constituents involved in the school community feel that they have a voice?
27. Have all stakeholders united around the basic purposes of the school?
28. Is the principal providing a source of continuous encouragement to staff and students?
29. Are problems addressed in systematic, timely ways?
30. Is the principal in control of his or her schedule, or does he or she simply respond to events?
31. Does the principal inspire support, confidence, and goodwill among staff members, students, and caregivers?

These evaluative criteria could be extended to a much longer list. As important as these indicators may be, however, they are all subordinate to improving children's learning. If achievement is rising, a principal may be considered doing a good job without meeting these criteria. If achievement is down, then meeting all these criteria will not be sufficient to compensate for the school's failure and his or her accountability.

In addition to his or her own evaluative criteria, the star principal is concerned with the criteria applied to staff members and students. These criteria should be open, public knowledge—and understood by those to whom they are applied. There should be valid means for assessing these criteria. They should be ranked from most to least important. Applying these guidelines will enable the principal to develop evaluation criteria for school secretaries or custodians as well as for the professional staff.

In addition to evaluating his or her own work habits and professional skills and those of others in the school, a third type of evaluation applies to the total school program. The evaluative indicators cited above can be developed into behavioral indicators for judging the progress of the school. Schools serving children in poverty are typically characterized by specific ethnic and cultural constituencies;

if a school is predominantly serving one cultural group, it will develop certain characteristics on which it can and should be evaluated. Qualities may include, for example, the use of language assistants or parents serving as ombudsmen. Other schools serving a diverse population can develop indicators specific to meeting the needs of several cultural groups. In short, an effective school reflects its particular community. Even if students are all bused in from different areas, the community is represented by the children's backgrounds and cultures and not by the immediate geographic neighborhood.

Evaluation and Facilitation

As both evaluator and facilitator, even the best principal finds evaluation a tall order. In much of his or her behavior, the principal is a source of support, a remover of obstacles, and a creator of conditions that facilitate learning. He or she gains information by listening and solves problems by being perceived as fair and impartial. He or she provides constant, nonjudgmental encouragement. Yet the principal is also the school's authority figure, legally and actually responsible for ensuring that the school meets its objectives. At some point, the principal must judge the quality of everyone's performance. In supervising teachers, it takes two people to communicate opposing perceptions: "Hey, I'm on your side" and "You better come clean, or I'll really punish you." We apply this "good cop, bad cop" principle in mentoring beginning teachers. The mentor teacher provides only help and encouragement and does not make formal assessments. A separate supervisor evaluates whether or not to recommend the beginner for certification. If the mentor performed both functions, the teacher being supervised would stop asking for help and would be loath to reveal weaknesses. Knowing an individual will be making important judgments about us makes us vulnerable and therefore less willing to be forthcoming.

The principal has to achieve these dual functions of providing support and being judgmental simultaneously. Some principals resolve this dilemma by emphasizing one role and giving up the other. They try to function as a full-time "buddy" or a full-time "boss." Star principals, however, manage both roles successfully. Socializing with teachers for whom they will also file annual teacher-evaluation reports requires a high level of human-relations ability. The unreflective principal does not understand that his or her difficulty relating to others comes from having to be both supportive *and* judgmental. The effective principal is well aware of this challenge and shapes his or her behavior to the situation.

Case 7: Process or Product Criteria

After lengthy, difficult negotiations, a teacher contract has been hammered out in Great City. The contract includes a new form for principals to use in evaluating teachers annually. The old form was a simple card on which the principal checked "Superior," "Satisfactory," or "Unsatisfactory." Each year, every teacher would be informed of the rating, and the card would be filed in his or her personnel record. This year, a new, more elaborate system has been adopted. The new form calls for the principal to assess 15 items as either "Satisfactory" or "Needs Improvement." The items on the new teacher-evaluation form are:

1. Complies with school policies.
2. Participates on school committees.
3. Maintains school materials/equipment.
4. Makes time available to students for extra help.
5. Achieves promptness/attendance criteria.
6. Communicates courteously.
7. Completes record keeping and paperwork.
8. Keeps up with new content.
9. Sustains good parental relations.
10. Follows curriculum guides.
11. Maintains classroom discipline.
12. Uses appropriate instructional methods.
13. Dresses professionally/appropriately.
14. Grades fairly.
15. Participates in staff development.

In much of his or her behavior, the principal is a source of support, a remover of obstacles, and a creator of conditions that facilitate learning. Yet the principal is also the school's authority figure.

On the same evening that the school board unanimously accepted the new teacher contract, including the new teacher-rating system, it discussed raising school achievement in the district. When Howard Grey was hired, the new superintendent received two charges: "Raise achievement, and cut the number of dropouts." On this evening, the school board asked the superintendent what steps he was going to take to implement these goals now that he had been in office three months. Grey promised that a plan would be in place by next month's board meeting.

The next day was Grey's monthly meeting with the 157 school principals of the district. He put aside the planned agenda and spoke for 45 minutes on the need

Chapter 8

to raise student achievement. Grey noted that there was ample time to prepare students for achievement tests in May. He made it clear that nothing was more important than student learning, that everything should be done to foster learning, and that all obstacles to learning should be removed. Grey finished his address by smashing his hand on the podium and shouting, "I plan to hold every principal accountable for raising his or her school's test scores. I expect each of you to hold every teacher accountable for raising every classroom's achievement. There will be no alternative to raising scores. That's it! Period! Meeting adjourned!"

Jerry Morton, principal of Jefferson Middle School, returned to his school convinced that the Great City School District was finally committed to raising test scores. As principal of a middle school, he would also be responsible for cutting dropouts. His students would be expected to show up in high school and not "disappear."

For the next six months, Morton constantly reminded Jefferson's faculty members: "Achievement tests are coming. Get students ready." In May, the tests were administered, and Jefferson students made modest improvements. Morton breathed a sigh of relief, believing his job was safe for another year.

In June, Morton filled out his teacher-rating forms. His lowest rating was for Fred Brown, an eighth-grade mathematics teacher. Of the 15 items, Brown received a "Needs Improvement" rating on 12. Morton also added, "Uses profanity in the classroom."

In a personal conference just before summer break, Brown informed Morton that he was filing a grievance against him with the teachers' union. Brown also stated that he had retained a lawyer and was suing Morton for harassment. The essence of Brown's complaint was that his classes surpassed (1) previous years' test scores, (2) the average class gains for the school as a whole, (3) eighth-grade gains in math for the middle school serving gifted students, and (4) eighth-grade math scores for the district as a whole. Brown prepared charts and graphs with elaborate statistical analyses supporting these assertions. Morton could not fully comprehend the charts but understood them well enough to know that Brown was essentially correct in his use of statistical data. Brown also informed Morton that every student in his five classes—147 in all—was going on to high school, which could be readily checked with district attendance records next September.

Morton explained to Brown that he had followed procedures in evaluating him and that no items on the rating scale dealt with raising test scores or having zero dropouts. Brown responded that Morton should stand up for raising students' achievement and not make "a silly set of items" more important than students' learning. As the conference proceeded, Brown stated he was going to add a charge of discrimination, because Morton had rated teachers with lower test scores higher than himself—the teacher with the highest scores.

After the meeting, Morton wondered whether Grey would support him or Brown. Would he need his own lawyer, or would the school system's lawyer defend him? He also mused about the security of his position as principal.

Analysis

Mr. Morton, like all principals, must understand the difference between process and product criteria. The official teacher-evaluation form contained only process items, while the school board and superintendent identified demonstrable changes in children's learning and behavior as the school's product. Thus, the written teacher-evaluation form did not align with the stated goals of the school system.

Such situations are frequent, and principals must be aware of the bottom line. If the school board is serious about holding the superintendent accountable, then it can be expected the superintendent will hold principals accountable as well. The principal should have predicted that the items on this teacher-evaluation form would not be sufficient. Brown's case was inevitable. It may not always be as dramatic, but teachers who score low on process items may have children who learn more as measured by standardized tests.

Understanding the criteria of evaluation, Morton should have anticipated this problem. Once he saw that the items on the teacher-evaluation form did not include raising test scores or lowering the number of dropouts—the system's highest stated priorities—he needed to take action. First, Morton needed to communicate to all constituencies—superiors as well as subordinates—potential problems that might have arisen from not aligning the teacher-evaluation form with the system's stated goals. Second, he needed to initiate procedures for adding student achievement and retaining students to the teachers' evaluations. For districts in which teachers' unions resist connecting teacher evaluation with children's achievement-test scores, teachers can be required to create portfolios as evidence of their children's work and learning. Teachers cannot be adequately evaluated without some reference to children's learning. In this case, Morton must now backtrack and hope that he can still accomplish the task of expanding the teacher evaluation to include evidence of student learning.

Chapter 8

Discussion Questions

1. In this case, is Mr. Morton representing the views of the administration down to staff members, the teachers up to the central office, both, or neither?

2. In filling out Mr. Brown's evaluation, what positive and negative messages was Morton sending to other faculty members?

3. What process and product criteria is Superintendent Grey likely to use in evaluating Morton?

Chapter 9

Decision Making

Everyone favors democratic decision making—until it comes to deciding an issue in which he or she has a vested interest.

The notion that the principal can function as an independent decision maker is dangerous. The more important the issue, the greater the likelihood that the principal will need additional information and wider consultation with others.

Many of the problems presented to the principal do not require decisions at all. It is common for staff members, students, and parents holding differing views to present their issues as "either-or" choices. Confronting the principal with disagreements, they request immediate decisions supporting one side or the other. In most cases, the wise principal simply redefines the problem, offering a solution that makes the dispute a nonissue. If this cannot be done, the principal redefines the problem to present additional alternatives to the two disputants' options. In cases requiring immediate action, the principal makes a decision then follows up on how the situation will be handled in the future.

It is natural for people to push the principal into making more and more decisions independently. The principal should be exerting pressure in the opposite direction, making staff members, teachers, and students responsible participants also accountable for decisions.

Unsophisticated principals often become trapped by the use of time pressures. For example, it is ten minutes before class, and a teacher must use the copying machine to duplicate a test. At the same time, the principal has ordered a secretary to copy a document in time for the 8 A.M. mail pickup for the central office. The teacher and the secretary meet at the copying machine and argue about whose work should be done first. The naive principal who regards problems such as who has priority at the copying machine as unimportant or nonsensical is headed for deep trouble. These types of problems can be perceived as extremely important to the participants, who define them in personal terms rather than by reflecting on school

Chapter 9

priorities. The principal who regards any interpersonal problem as trivial is seriously mistaken. Such insensitivity will inevitably lead staff members to perceive that decisions are made capriciously or, even worse, that decisions are always made against them, even if this is not the case. Effective principals avoid this trap in two ways: (1) they never assume a decision they have made independently, immediately, and without consultation to be a trivial matter; and (2) they always solicit feedback from participants and, if necessary, plan with them how to handle similar situations in the future.

Analyzing Decision Making

One way for the principal to analyze his or her decision-making process is to note decisions briefly at the end of each day for a week. By Friday afternoon, there will be as many as 100 decisions if he or she has captured only a part of them.

The principal should write down each decision in one brief sentence, marking each one with an "S" or an "I" to indicate whether the decision favors the "system" or the "individual," respectively. "S" decisions uphold school rules, traditions, and policies, thereby preventing individuals from doing something they wanted to get done. Sometimes the only rationale available to a principal for "S" decisions is to say, "If I let you do this, everyone will want to do it." On the other hand, "I" decisions support the individual's request that an exception be made to a school rule, tradition, or policy. In many cases, "I" decisions circumvent rules. Star principals make very few "S" decisions. When they believe students will benefit or a teacher's hard work should be supported, they make "I" decisions. These principals perceive their role as protecting individuals doing well or trying to do well rather than supporting an irrational or insensitive bureaucracy.

Just as star principals make as few "S" decisions as possible, they also seek to make as few rules as possible. It is common in schools to create rules for events that rarely occur. Any single event seems to push some principals into establishing a binding rule.

Several years ago, for example, a new school was built featuring a central library and computer lab with doors leading into every classroom. It was a marvelous example of how architecture can support a school program rather than a school program adjusting to the limitations of a building. During the first week in the new school, a few students stole some library books. Immediately, a decision was made that all classroom doors into the library must be kept locked. Only one door was left open for all students and school personnel to enter and leave the library. The architectural advantage was lost in the very first week of the school's life. Now, 25 years later, the situation remains the same. No classroom doors into the library have ever been opened. An incompetent principal, pressured by an overreacting librarian and a few teachers who did not want two doors into their classrooms, decided to protect some library books rather than the learning opportunities of thousands of students for decades to come. Examples like these abound in schools, because the culture fosters rule making for the misbehavior of a few while sacrificing the general well-being of all.

Star principals are both people-oriented and task-oriented. They achieve the stated goals and simultaneously build strong, positive human relations with staff members of varying personalities.

Star principals make exceptions and resist making rules because a small percentage of students misbehave. Weak principals create new rules in response to single events. They are insensitive to the often burdensome nature of the school's bureaucracy.

Another important decision-making area for principals involves improving human relations and achieving the stated objectives of the school. Principals who want to be loved do not think in terms of tasks to be accomplished. Conversely, task-oriented principals are frequently insensitive to the needs of the people involved. Single-dimension principals are concerned with either making teachers and staff members happy or achieving the school's objectives. Star principals are both people-oriented and task-oriented. They achieve the stated goals—higher achievement, fewer dropouts, and greater parental involvement—and simultaneously build strong, positive human relations with staff members of varying personalities.

Decision Making and Success

The reason there are successful schools within failing school systems relates to the process of decision making. Decisions made at the system level seldom impact the work of classroom teachers directly. By the time most system policies and decisions reach the teacher, they have been strained through several layers of the bureaucracy at the central office. Various administrators, fiscal officers, and lawyers have made sure that any decision reached will not jeopardize their own power bases.

Chapter 9

When a decision reaches the school level, the principal then decides whether he or she can live with it and how to interpret the decision to the school staff. It is like a game: the decision is handed along from person to person and purposely changed to please the next transmitter. The *coup de grace* is that the system usually does not have the span of control either to monitor or to enforce its decisions at every level. With hundreds of schools and thousands of classrooms, there are no rewards for implementing top-level decisions and no penalties for ignoring them. The system can "decide" and then simply hope that a policy decision will be implemented at all levels.

On the other hand, the school building is still within the principal's span of control. Even without observing every classroom, decisions made at the school level can and usually do impact the life of the classroom. There are also usually consequences for staff members who comply with school decisions and those who do not. Individual schools are, in large measure, isolated from the main bureaucracy of the central office. They are connected only by some weak strands—a monthly meeting between principals and the superintendent; a small school-discretionary budget that does not alter the general enrollment-based financial structure, and a series of projects that do not impact the school's basic curriculum and can be terminated when funding runs out. In effect, the school operates without the central office, and the central office operates without real control over the schools. Indeed, the more detached the individual school becomes from the chaotic central bureaucracy, the greater its opportunity to be more responsive and effective.

Case 8: Whose Rights?

Karen Jones was assigned a teaching load of five seventh- and eighth-grade language arts classes in the King Middle School. New to the district and the school, Jones faced the following incident during the second week in the fall semester.

Jones had just started her second-hour class when the door to her classroom burst open. An individual, later identified as her estranged husband, entered and ran to Jones's desk, where he began examining the contents of her purse. Jones and the intruder began an argument that quickly became loud and violent. The intruder began striking Jones, and the teacher from an adjoining classroom, Joe Hart, entered the room. When Hart tried to intercede, the intruder struck him several times. Many students ran out of the classroom into the hallway. Safety aides entered the classroom and physically restrained the intruder. City police arrived and removed him. Both Jones and her estranged husband were required to appear in court the next day.

That afternoon, several parents called the principal, Bill Murphy, demanding that he improve school safety. The superintendent's office called several times to ascertain the facts. Local media arrived at the school for an interview with the principal. Murphy explained that the intruder slipped past a strict school-security system with a group of visitors from the Red Cross.

That evening, Murphy received calls from an attorney representing Hart, a representative of the local teachers' union, and the assistant superintendent for administrative services. Pressure was building for the principal to make a decision. Should Jones be transferred to protect students' safety? Should Jones's right to remain in her classroom be upheld? How does the principal go about making such critical decisions?

Analysis

Emergency situations are the best test of what an individual truly believes about decision making. Under the stressful pressure of having to take action, Mr. Murphy's decision and the explanation he offers for making that decision provide a window into his perceptions. What does the principal believe are the ultimate values to be preserved in this situation? Is it children's safety? Is it the rights of the teacher?

The process the principal follows in making this decision will indicate whether he believes that decisions should be based on as much information as possible or serve as a test of his status and power. The weakest basis for decision making is to act on incomplete data and seek little or no input. The individual who acts without the necessary information mistakenly regards seeking data as a sign of weakness.

Before the principal in this case can decide that the safety of the children requires transferring Ms. Jones out of the school, he must consider several issues regarding this complex case:

★ What are the teacher-transfer polices in the district?

★ Has a case like this occurred previously? If so, how was it resolved?

★ If a transfer of Jones takes a few weeks, would she continue to be paid? If so, whose budget would cover her salary?

★ Is there a vacancy in another school available for Jones? If so, must the principal of that school agree to receive her?

- ★ Is it necessary for Jones to agree to the transfer?

- ★ Will this incident appear on Jones's school record?

- ★ Does the bargaining agreement between the school district and the teachers' union address this issue? In districts without teacher contracts, does the teachers' association address such concerns?

- ★ Will transferring Jones lead to a formal grievance or a lawsuit being filed?

- ★ What problems might arise with other teachers, children, or parents from transferring Jones?

Each of these issues requires thorough but rapid data gathering by the principal. As if this course were not sufficiently difficult, consider the issues the principal must address if he decides *not* to transfer Jones:

- ★ How does the principal ensure that the estranged husband will not come onto school property in the future?

- ★ Is it possible to work out a better security system for screening visitors to the school?

- ★ Is a better emergency system needed to handle similar situations?

- ★ Are resources available for improving the school's security?

- ★ How will the principal explain the plan under which Jones will stay in the building to parents, teachers, staff members, and children who feel unsafe?

- ★ Will keeping Jones as a teacher make the school district vulnerable to lawsuits from individuals who believe safety has been compromised and insufficient action was taken to remedy the situation?

- ★ Will keeping Jones cause an increase in insurance costs for everyone who works in the building?

- ★ Will it be possible to retain Jones if *she* wants to transfer?

Obviously, all of these questions cannot be addressed in one day. Still, it will be necessary for Murphy to find answers as quickly as possible. In addition, the broader issues that must be clarified immediately are: (1) what legal issues are involved; and (2) what would be best for the students.

The principal must understand that he acts only after consulting with others who can provide essential information. Even with emergency decisions such as this one, the principal can act after securing as much information as possible on the first day and then continue the process of subsequent data gathering. He must solicit input from others and listen carefully to the views of all stakeholders who would be affected by the decision.

Just as it would be unwise for the principal to act alone and immediately without gaining more data and suggestions, it would be equally disastrous for the principal to abdicate his or her authority. For example, calling a teachers' meeting and having them vote on whether Jones should remain in the building would be just as great an indicator of incompetence as not seeking more data and input. Though teachers have an important voice in this matter, they are not the only constituency involved; nor do they possess the necessary legal and policy backgrounds.

On the very first day, the principal should be able to state, "I am presently taking the following action for these reasons." After listing several steps, he can add, "This action is subject to change as we determine more about the situation." Ultimately, Murphy will be held responsible and accountable for making the decision in this case, but he must first consult with others, gather data, and consider his options.

Discussion Questions

1. List the decisions Mr. Murphy must make. With whom, if anyone, might he consult before making each decision?
2. What written records should Murphy make in documenting this problem?
3. What is the ultimate value Murphy should seek to preserve in resolving this problem?

Chapter 10

Fallibility

Developed through life experience rather than by attending a university class on school administration for twelve consecutive Thursday nights, character is manifested by one's ability to give and get respect. A principal who lacks this ability will fail.

For children to learn, they must feel free to try new things. In an effective mathematics class, for example, children are encouraged to explore every solution without penalty. The desired atmosphere is one of encouragement and teamwork—youngsters help each other and never deride others or make fun of failed attempts. Moreover, the teacher must be willing to make attempts and admit mistakes. Values are taught through modeling appropriate behaviors rather than by direct instruction.

For teachers to admit their fallibility requires school leaders to do the same. The chain of influence that creates a school climate—whether positive or negative—starts with the principal, influences the teachers, and impacts the children. A principal who believes that there are no dumb questions, only better solutions, helps develop a positive school learning climate. A school leader who engages in simple honesty regarding his or her own mistakes engenders the same responses in everyone else. Admitting errors is a sign of strength; reluctance to show fallibility is a sign of weakness.

It is not difficult for a school leader to determine whether he or she has created a positive school climate. One indicator of such a learning atmosphere is that teachers, acting in a professional and courteous way, feel free to criticize. If the principal is open to suggestions, he or she inevitably will receive them. Conveying the concept that all wisdom does not reside at the top creates a second benefit: school staff members feel as if "we are all in this together." A good idea, a better way, or even a workable solution can come from any source.

Star Principals' Ideology

An effective leader must have an ideology characteristic of star principals in schools serving children in poverty. This ideology derives from a set of beliefs that predispose the principal to act in certain ways. Without the undergirding ideology, the actions themselves would be hollow behaviors. They could not be influential unless they represented the principal's true beliefs. Conversely, the principal's genuine beliefs would be of no value if they were not also translated into actions that bring them to life. The ideology combines both a set of beliefs and a set of actions demonstrating them.

Where and how does such an ideology develop? Beliefs result from individuals reflecting upon and extracting learnings from their life experiences. Formal university training may teach examples of leadership behaviors, but it is unlikely to transmit the belief system that must undergird it. Training can only be of value if the candidates have been carefully screened and selected as individuals predisposed to believe the ideology of star principals. It is possible to train candidates with the appropriate beliefs to perform in ways star principals do. Without such selection, the formal training of school administrators is essentially a set of university courses that does not predict future behavior of those certified as leaders.

A Question of Training

Does graduate training in educational administration improve U.S. schools? Haller, Brent, and McNamara (1997), researchers engaged in training school administrators, set out to answer that question. First, they discovered that the United States is one of few countries requiring graduate training for school administrators. An examination of other industrialized countries without such requirements, however, revealed that U.S. schools are not administered any better. Second, though private schools fair better than public schools, most have no formal requirements for administrator training. Third, the educators examined qualitative data from a professor of school administration. For example, asked if he had used the theories and concepts he taught at the university, the professor was forced to answer "no." Fourth, they surveyed practicing principals about the value of formal preparation on actual practice and found that more experienced principals were more dissatisfied with the training. In fact, all principals surveyed noted many irrelevancies in professional training. Fifth, upon examining specific attempts to connect principals' training and practice, they found no correlation between how principals were rated in training and in practice. Haller et al. (1997, 227) concluded the literature search by stating, "Overall . . . there is little evidence that graduate training increases the effectiveness of school managers."

The three experts then examined a sample of 6,341 schools. Independent variables were the degrees obtained by the administrators and their major fields of study. The dependent variable was school effectiveness based on five indices—leader, climate, order, policy, and help—as assessed by school staffs. Using multivariate analysis to assess principals' training on school effectiveness, Haller et al. (1997, 225) concluded their study by noting:

> Taken collectively, graduate programs in educational administration seem to have little or no influence on the attributes that characterize effective schools. . . . To the extent that these attributes are, in fact, causes of valued school outcomes, evidence that graduate training in school administration has no effect on them is evidence that the training is irrelevant to the goals we seek. . . . This research casts further doubt on the presumption that graduate training for school administrators has improved U.S. schools. . . . It is not evident that we should require more training or even different training. Perhaps we should require less. Or none at all.

The Right Candidates

My experience regarding the value of formal training is more optimistic than the views of Haller, Brent, and McNamara, provided the right individuals—those with the appropriate ideology—are selected as the candidates. My second proviso is that the training must not be limited to formal college coursework; it must emphasize an on-the-job internship in which the administrator in residence can be coached by a star principal.

This leadership dimension of fallibility is an especially appropriate dimension around which to have a discussion. Selection—not training—is the process for identifying candidates who will likely believe in and accept their fallibility as a positive attribute. Having identified individuals with such a predisposition, it then becomes possible to coach them on-the-job in how to use this attribute to enhance school climate.

Case 9: Censorship

Dave Dominick has a new agenda for his second year as principal of West High School. At the top of his list is cutting down on dropouts and raising student achievement. He has spent all summer on strategies for improving instruction throughout the school; when Labor Day arrives, Dominick is ready.

The first issue of the student newspaper, *Now,* is published in the second week of the school term. It includes movie reviews and an editorial section on whether teenagers should be barred from seeing movies that receive certain ratings. The articles include examples of profane language used in these movies. On the day the paper is distributed, Dominick's telephone begins to jingle. It seems every parent in the community is an avid reader of *Now,* and more than a few are upset with the movie language quoted in the issue. Some calls—not many—are from parents expressing approval that the school paper is sufficiently open-minded to print these words. Most of the calls, including several from influential community religious leaders, express shock and disappointment.

Almost all conclude with the question, "What are you going to do about this?"

Dominick and his assistants soon become aware of another problem. When teachers want to remove a student from their classes, they fill out a card called a "64" and send him or her to the principal's office. Over the course of a week, an unusual number of 64 cards list swearing as the reason for requesting the student be suspended for one, two, or three days. It does not take much investigation by the assistant principals to determine that many of these words—seven, to be exact—are in the *Now* article explaining what causes some movies to have an adult rating.

Because this same issue has cropped up in two forms at the outset of the school year, Dominick decides he had better nip it in the bud. He calls a school assembly for the follow-ing Friday and issues a new "no nonsense" school policy against using any of these seven specific words in oral or written form on school grounds, at any school event away from school, or in any manner associated with any school publication, communication, or function. At the assembly, Dominick actually states the seven words and informs students that anyone using these words will receive an automatic three-day suspension. In the course of this presentation, Dominick also announces that *Now* will not be published until further notice.

The community newspaper was informed that the school assembly would take

> *Weak principals never admit mistakes. They regard acknowledgment of error—particularly in public—as a sign of weakness. They stonewall and, by persisting in the error, escalate and perpetuate the matter even further.*

place and sent a reporter to cover it. Dominick gives the reporter permission to sit in on the assembly, because he wants to show the community that this is a serious matter and he means business. The next issue of the community newspaper features Dominick on the front page. The reporter's article features a photograph of the principal reading the seven forbidden words at the student assembly. The newspaper does not actually print the words but gives clues, noting much tittering and laughter among the students during Dominick's presentation on the evils of profanity.

Rather than squash the issue, the situation has become worse. Students are now mouthing the words without speaking them, writing them around the school, or writing the first and last letters of the words and leaving the other letters blank.

The issue has caught the imagination of the student body for a variety of reasons. For the staff on the school newspaper, it has become a students' rights issue: "All we did was report and analyze the movie rating system." For a few students, it has become an easy way to get "a three-day pass"—just say one of the magic words. For the majority of youngsters, the issue has become a standing joke. Rather than learn a moral lesson—profanity is bad—they have started playing games. They use the words more than ever, but not in ways for which they can be punished. The list of seven terms has been easily memorized. Students now fool around with each other by stating, "I never called you a six. You're just a rotten four." It is clear to everyone that the problem is not going away.

West High's teachers are upset because they feel Dominick and the school administration have allowed the student staff of *Now* to "put one over on them" and publish an edition without any oversight by the teacher editorial committee. Last year's teacher advisors never checked any of this year's stories—their assignment as editors ended in June, and they assumed that new teacher advisors would be appointed in September. In the confusion of starting a new semester, new teacher advisors had not yet been appointed. Somehow, *Now* went to press without any faculty oversight.

Parents are upset, because the story in the community newspaper pokes fun at the helplessness of the school at stemming the problem of their children's profanity. The assistant principals are upset because of the large number of class suspensions they must handle.

Most of the students are having a grand time playing games with the forbidden words and tweaking school authority. They know the school's leaders are not interested in enforcing their own stated rules. Dominick feels caught in a trap, realizing that he has let the situation get away from him. He is also starting to feel resentful and frustrated at being in no position to begin his instructional-improvement initiative.

Analysis

Effective principals make mistakes. Yet when they do err, they admit it and seek to put the matter behind them as expeditiously as possible. Weak principals never admit mistakes. They regard acknowledgment of error—particularly in public—as a sign of weakness. They stonewall and, by persisting in the error, escalate and perpetuate the matter even further. The ultimate value to be preserved in the West High School situation is not the principal "saving face." Mr. Dominick will demonstrate greater strength by admitting he did not handle the situation well.

First, Dominick should have appointed teachers to the newspaper editorial staff before school ended the preceding June. Second, he could have had the assistant principals conduct a quick survey of teachers to determine if the rash of "64s" at the opening of the school year was related to the *Now* story or if something else was going on with students. Third, Dominick *never* should have put himself in the position of reciting the profane words in a public assembly. Nor should he have allowed the community newspaper into the school to cover him reading the forbidden words. Fourth, "freedom of the press" is a nonissue. U.S. courts have made it clear that students in school do not enjoy the same rights as citizens in the greater society. If, in the judgment of school authorities, the safety of students or their best educational interests are to be served by enforcing a dress code, censoring a newspaper, or demanding certain forms of behavior and communication, then school authorities have that right and responsibility. Dominick might have handled this situation better either by holding a meeting with the editors of *Now* and getting them to agree to print a retraction or by suspending them for breaking existing school rules on using profanity in the newspaper.

After ascertaining the facts, Dominick could have met with parents and explained his mistakes in allowing the newspaper to appear without faculty editing. He should take responsibility and admit his errors to parents, faculty, and staff members.

Dominick will need to prepare a written statement on the school's suspension policy. He should make this statement after consultation with teachers, staff members, parents, and students. He should also review school district policy before issuing any further statements.

Chapter 10

Discussion Questions

1. In considering Mr. Dominick's behavior, what has he done that has been most detrimental to the students?

2. What might Dominick do that is now most likely to put an end to this episode?

3. What lessons are there in this episode for the principal seeking to diminish the use of profanity?

Chapter 11

Administrative Style for Implementing Change

The most enduring and impermeable school practices were never approved by anyone; they are the unchallenged rituals that schools simply inherit. Star principals hold these rituals up to public scrutiny.

The 120 largest school systems in the United States offer a plethora of special projects. Some type of federal or state initiative is, in fact, commonplace in a majority of the schools. Most urban districts also offer self-funded projects, programs, and initiatives. These "great ideas" for improving the education of children in poverty may originate with school board members, superintendents, central office administrators, or community groups. Projects oftentimes are initiated by local businesses or in response to prompts from news media. In some cases, area universities receive grants to partner with the local school district. Occasionally, with greater school-based management and the designation of particular buildings as specialty schools, projects and initiatives may emanate from a particular school faculty and parent group.

Projectitis

Urban school systems suffer from "projectitis." Among the symptoms of this affliction are the following: little planning or preparation time at the initiation of the project; little or no training of teachers and staff who will be responsible for offering the project; little or no consideration of how the addition of the new project will affect the basic educational program of the school; little or no funds, personnel, or plans for evaluating the new project; no attempt to align the new program with the district's standardized tests; no planning on how to institutionalize, administer, and pay for the project when it expires; and no planning for sequencing projects and programs in elementary, middle, and high school buildings. Moreover, schools fail to offer the project for a long enough period to realize or assess its value or impact. An analogue to this situation would be an extremely ill patient receiving several dozen treatments simultaneously. If by some miracle there were an improvement in the patient's condition, his or her progress would remain unattributable to any particular treatment.

In its disparate efforts to improve the education being offered children in poverty, urban schools grasp at every straw. Frequently, projects and programs have contradictory impacts and effects. Some initiatives, for example, use behavior modification as the process of learning. Other programs are based on intrinsic motivation and meeting idiosyncratic learner needs. New projects based on team learning might be offered to students already in programs emphasizing individual differences and abilities. Many students in urban schools are taught by both highly directive authoritarian teachers *and* by educators whose instruction depends on student experiences. What is the effect of some teachers regarding students as empty vessels to be filled and other teachers regarding them as the primary source of all relevant knowledge?

These are just a few of the problems caused by projectitis in urban school systems. A concomitant problem is a decrease in the number of regular classroom teachers and a marked increase in the number of teachers who specialize in a particular program, teaching methodology, or a new approach to a particular subject matter. When programs of sex education, antiviolence, and other social issues are added to core subjects, the problem of projectitis compounds. The number of teaching specialists hired to improve, augment, or change the regular curriculum sometimes equals the number of regular teachers. One unanticipated effect of projectitis is the de facto decision that add-on projects and programs constitute a better school-improvement strategy than simply cutting class size in half. School change agents pushing their own particular projects often do not consider the best interests of the total school district. Lowering class size would be a more reasonable and effective school-improvement strategy than continually adding projects and programs that cause chaos and no discernable effects.

Dealing with Faculty and Staff

Because superintendents in large urban school districts turnover every two or three years and those in small urban districts last only a year or so longer, the urban principal must deal with temporary superiors who act as permanent employees. The principal must wholeheartedly seek to implement the current superintendent's initiatives, knowing he or she likely will not be around long enough to take credit or blame for the initiative. The principal, therefore, must deal with faculty and staff members in different ways.

Some teachers will react to new projects by stating, "Wait a year, and it will go away." Unfortunately, they are too often correct. As funding changes or dries up because a school board member leaves or a superintendent departs, a particular initiative may be abandoned. Frequently, the number one priority in September is gone by the start of the next school year. Federal- and state-funded initiatives compound this problem with the assumption that deep-seated needs of children in poverty can be remedied by an educational injection of "something" that takes a year or less to implement. Thus, the first problem the principal faces with a new district initiative is countering the impact of naysayers on his or her staff who warn other teachers not to waste their enthusiasm on a "here today, gone tomorrow" project. In effect, the principal must work hard and with total commitment to counter negators, knowing full well they may be correct.

Other teachers will remain open to another initiative if the principal can convince them it will really help children. He or she must involve the school faculty in every step of the new initiative, from planning to evaluation. Unless staff members accept the project as their own, they will not make it work. The most fundamental truism of school change is that *no innovation* is teacher proof. No new material, equipment, textbook, school reorganization, media project, computer program, teaming method, or instructional system can withstand the impact of teachers who implement the change with less than total commitment and full understanding. Changes teachers

The surest way for a principal to resist projectitis is to raise student achievement scores. The principal can then argue that he or she should be given more time to stay on the right track with the current program.

believe in work; the others fail. The principal, therefore, has no choice: He or she cannot simply inform teachers of their next project, nor just relate objectives and allow only input with how goals will be implemented. Staff members must have a voice in every aspect of the initiative for it to be their own. Effective principals know this.

Chapter 11

Managing the Work Load

Once the principal realizes some level of buy-in among a critical mass of the faculty, his or her real job has begun. He or she must make sure the new project does not increase the workload of the more cooperative teachers while leaving the blockers and naysayers with a lighter load. One of the unfortunate consequences of projectitis is that some principals keep adding to the work of good teachers, who care the most and work the hardest. This approach leaves educators who do the poorest jobs and who tend not to volunteer or be identified as good enough for special projects with relatively less and less to do. Poor principals exploit better teachers and let poor teachers do the same old things. In such a situation, most teachers soon decide to be regarded as less-than-great educators, if only to be left alone.

The function of the effective principal as a change agent is to manage workloads, offering incentives rather than disincentives for participation in desired change efforts. One way is to build in planning and evaluation time. In addition, cooperative staff members should not have to spend more after-school time as volunteers; they should receive payment for extra work time. Recognition and encouragement are also rewards. Ultimately, the most powerful reward for good teachers is that the students they teach do better as a result of the new program or project.

The role of the principal in urban schools is of critical importance when it comes to new initiatives. He or she must involve staff members in determining which projects to undertake, how projects should be implemented, obstacles that must be removed for innovations to work, methods for program evaluation, and how new initiatives should be integrated into the total school program. Only through cooperative planning with the faculty can these processes be performed successfully. The surest way for a principal to resist projectitis is to raise student achievement scores. The principal can then argue that he or she should be given more time to stay on the right track with the current program. In the face of stagnant or declining achievement scores, however, the principal and school become more vulnerable to an increased attack of projectitis.

Case 10: Discretionary Funds

Mary Parker has compiled a very successful record as a high school principal over an eight-year period. Under her leadership, the dropout rate has declined and a majority of graduates now go on to some form of postsecondary education. As a result, the central office has transferred Parker to South High School. The superintendent has placed this school on probation for low student achievement and an unsatisfactory school climate. The charge given Parker is to "turn it around." To reward Parker for her willingness to take on South High, the superintendent has given the principal $250,000 in discretionary school funds.

Getting the building under control must be the first order of business. During the previous year, students and teachers were attacked in the school and on school grounds. Many students report being afraid for their personal safety and being under stress because of an inability to protect their belongings and money.

At a news media event prior to Labor Day, the superintendent announces Parker's appointment as South High's principal. He also reveals that she will have $250,000 at her disposal for school improvement.

In September, Parker meets with several of the school's constituencies. First, a committee of teachers explains that faculty members have given their lives to South High and will continue to do so. Committee members believe, however, that they are working under desperate conditions that absolutely must be changed. They urge the installation of television cameras in all corridors, stairwells, study halls, the cafeteria, and rooms not patrolled by safety aides. The cost of the cameras, monitors, and wiring is approximately $250,000.

A group of representatives from local businesses also meets with Parker. The business leaders suggest that many South High students believe they will never have the chance to land a decent job. As a result, pupils see little reason to expend much effort in school and fall prey to gangs and others with ideas on how to "make it" in life. The business community ran a highly successful pilot project at the school during the preceding year, connecting students to the world of work. Pupils worked part-time for pay while learning and practicing computer skills. The business leaders now have a plan to make the program available to any South High student that meets some basic skills and maintains a good record of punctuality, attendance, and attitude. They offer to match Parker's $250,000 with an equal amount in private funds to make the program a reality.

Curriculum directors from the central office are yet another constituency to visit Parker. They indicate a strong need for upgrading the school's study program. They note that there are inadequate computers, television monitors, science equipment, art supplies, and textbooks in almost every area of the curriculum. The directors explain that district schools can tap into government funds to meet all these needs. Indeed, for every dollar Parker invests, two dollars would be matched from local and state sources. In effect, by investing the $250,000, they would have $750,000 for much-needed supplies, equipment, learning materials, and textbooks. How can teachers teach and children learn without the necessary tools?

A fourth group that includes parents and community leaders visits Parker in September. A national foundation approached the school in the previous year to improve and strengthen parental involvement. This foundation has compiled a record of improving student achievement in impoverished schools by increasing the role of parents. In addition to learning how to help students with homework, parents would attend workshops on how to demonstrate support for their adolescents as well as how to fight drugs, teen pregnancy, and gang membership. Parents would be involved as aides—for pay—in a variety of school programs. Again, Parker is promised matching funds. Parents report past matched funds at a ratio of 3 to1 for similar projects. A representative of the foundation would be happy to come and make a presentation.

A fifth idea is not suggested by any constituency but emanates from Parker's previous experiences. The principal believes her success at the previous school came when she changed the school climate. A critical part of this change was having the school repainted inside and out. At South High, she would also need to install many new windows. She has already had several free consultations with landscape architects, masons, and roofers.

Parker has not yet discussed her ideas with anyone, but she is convinced that physical surroundings affect everyone's attitude and, until the students and teachers feel better about their surroundings, little else will be accomplished. South High's new principal believes the first step toward building school pride must be creating a building that is a source of pride.

Analysis

Ms. Parker's administrative style will determine what happens to the $250,000 in discretionary funds and how the decision is made. Her choices will affect relation-ships with each of the four constituencies, as well as with other constituencies not sufficiently organized to visit her but still observing and judging how she uses the funds.

Parker must now start a series of meetings in which she explains and justifies her decision to fix up the school. If she convinces the various constituencies to "do it her way" now, it will be less difficult to solve future problems. If Parker can reassure these constituencies that they will have a voice in determining future discretionary expenditures, she may succeed through this phase. Otherwise, she will begin her principalship by alienating the groups whose support and collaboration are vital to the school's—and her—success.

Discussion Questions

1. Given Ms. Parker's meetings with the four constituencies, what, if anything, is she now obligated to do?

2. What values and problems would result from representatives of the four constituencies meeting together?

3. Can a legitimate case be made for Parker making the final decision independently, without further consultation with any constituency?

Chapter 12

Administrator Relations with Parents and Community

What the wisest, best parents want for their children, the entire community must want for all its children. Star principals recognize and use these models of parental wisdom in building positive relations with the community.

In schools serving children in poverty, the principal will learn things about families and caregivers beyond his or her wildest imagination. Incidents of child abuse may be worse than those reported on television or depicted in fictional movies, magazines, or books. Cases of neglect abound as children are caught in fires, stifled in hot cars, and left unattended or forgotten. Parents and caregivers using drugs sacrifice the physical and emotional health of the children in their care. Furthermore, heinous activities pursued by young people may have been learned at home.

Despite individual cases of abuse and neglect, the principal must believe that parents want the very best for their children. Indeed, most parents want the same outcomes that a principal does for his or her own children. Unless the principal believes this point, he or she will not be able to relate to parents as individuals who seek the best education for their children.

Demonstrating Respect

Many of the parents, caregivers, and community members in schools serving children in poverty will not have the formal education or language skills of the principal. If the principal believes that these attributes are an appropriate measure of individuals' commitment or caring, he or she will be handicapped in building school relationships.

Whether the principal regards parents and caregivers as people of worth and as partners in an educational mission manifests in the way he or she speaks, stands, sits, greets, and interacts with them. Instances of such specific behaviors demonstrating courtesy are numerous. For example, the principal addressed by title must address other adults similarly and not by first name. Even the tone and level of voice is an indicator of one's perceptions. The parent, caregiver, or community member with whom the principal interacts must be treated as if he or she were prominent, affluent, highly experienced, and intelligent. If the principal is not clear on what respectful behaviors look like in action, he or she can visit the most prestigious, expensive private school in the area and sit in on a parent-teacher conference, a school meeting for parents, or a school social event to see how school leaders interact with people they respect and serve.

In sum, the principal leading a school in poverty must not focus on the minority of parents and caregivers harming their children but on the majority of individuals trying to be the best parents possible. He or she must build on this positive perception by demonstrating a sincere respect for parents and caregivers. The first obstacle the principal must overcome, therefore, is any perception that he or she leads from an elevated educational or social position.

Race, Ethnicity, and Class

The second obstacle the principal must overcome involves race, ethnicity, and class. If the principal's heritage is different from that of parents and caregivers, he or she must go through a period of proving ability and concern and establishing trust. A principal serving in a school with significant numbers of students for whom English is a second language can benefit from trying to learn the language. In most cases, the process of proving himself or herself is helped by the principal's participation in the community—at churches, ethnic festivals, social agencies, and community functions. Visiting students' homes also benefits principals in building trusting relationships. Principals who live outside the community should eat in local restaurants and patronize stores. These activities are important as well for principals of the same ethnic background but from a different class. In fact, it may be harder to establish trust for a principal of the same background who is perceived as "too good for us" than for a complete outsider. Trust-building is necessary for all principals. Unless the racial, ethnic, and class lines are broken, he or she will not be perceived as a partner.

Finding Balance

The third obstacle the principal faces is finding balance among the various community voices. Remember, "What the wisest, best parents want for their children, the entire community must want for all its children." Yet who decides the "wisest" and the "best"? A lengthy process of interactions among equals should help determine answers to these questions, reaching common agreements and creating a shared vision. Getting everyone on the same page takes time, effort, and mutual respect. The principal who is too tired, too important, or too busy for evening and weekend interactions will not build the necessary feelings of equality and trust. Without such a basis, common vision will not be developed.

Evaluating this third obstacle is easy. Has the principal achieved a balance of professional and community control? In some schools, principals still hold all the power and make the final decisions. Everyone votes, and then the principal decides. This traditional model will not work in the 21st century; parents, caregivers, and community members expect to be heard. At the other extreme, a group of community activists make all the important decisions, including how to use the school budget, which teachers to hire, who can be on the payroll as aides or substitutes, and whether the principal should be retained. As superintendents in one Midwestern great city told me, more than half of the day-to-day teacher substitutes paid by the district were found never to have appeared in any school building. Particular community-controlled schools were simply distributing money in their community by placing the names of individuals on the substitute payroll.

Between these extremes of principal autocracy and community chaos is the balance needed to operate an urban school successfully in an impoverished community. One way to ensure equity is by the leadership the principal exerts. He or she must make certain that school decisions are open and all constituencies have input in developing the criteria. When people understand the decision-making process, they are empowered in two ways: through their involvement and by being able to criticize the decisions. Actions discussed openly, then arrived at and shared openly, contribute to reaching a balance in determining how much control parents, caregivers, and community members should have. The second way the principal can achieve balance is by organizing the means to evaluate and reconsider decisions at a later date. A third task of the school leader in this process is to make certain that all "voices" are represented, including those of experts, and to recruit representatives of constituencies being overlooked.

The principal of a school serving children in poverty does not simply view parents as clients; rather, the total society is the client or recipient of the school's product. The school leader must view parents and caregivers as partners in the educative process. The greatest challenge the principal faces is making it a partnership among equals reaching balanced decisions. A useful checklist for determining a school's responsiveness to the needs of impoverished children and families is included below.

Checklist for Determining How Your School
Responds to Children and Families in Poverty

Yes__ No__   1. Are your staff members sensitive to the fact that many parents and caregivers regard them as well off or even affluent?

Yes__ No__   2. Do your staff members recognize and use the strengths of poor children and their families when offering classroom programs?

Yes__ No__   3. Do your teachers serve as role models by communicating respect for children and caregivers?

Yes__ No__   4. Are your staff members aware of the health human-service needs of the children in their classes?

Yes__ No__   5. Are your staff members aware of the health and human services actually being provided to the children in their classes?

Yes__ No__   6. Does the school maintain and disseminate a list of community agencies and programs serving poor children, including eligibility requirements and the particular services provided?

Yes__ No__   7. Are the privacy rights of children and their families scrupulously protected?

Yes__ No__   8. In emergency situations, can the school refer children and caregivers to agencies that supply food, clothing, and shelter?

Yes__ No__   9. Does the school have direct connections with juvenile authorities to follow up on cases of child abuse?

Yes__ No__   10. Are there provisions for children who cannot pay extra fees to participate in all required school activities and secure all necessary learning materials, including uniforms?

> *The school leader must view parents and caregivers as partners in the educative process. The greatest challenge the principal faces is making it a partnership among equals reaching balanced decisions.*

Yes__ No__   11. Are adult volunteers other than parents used in the school?

Yes__ No__   12. Does the school provide a way for teachers and caregivers to learn more about the world of work?

Yes__ No__   13. Have connections with local businesses been made to foster a school-to-work strand in the curriculum?

Yes__ No__   14. Is there a school-parent coordinator?

Yes__ No__   15. Has the school provided for parents' and caregivers' special language needs?

Yes__ No__   16. Do parent-community groups represent all segments of the community?

Yes__ No__   17. Is it expected that teachers will make home visits?

Yes__ No__   18. Are the cultural institutions in the community, including newspapers, businesses, and ethnic societies, visible in the school curriculum?

Yes__ No__   19. Do parents and caregivers have input on how they will participate in the school?

Yes__ No__   20. Is there a regular feedback mechanism for parents and caregivers to evaluate the school and their involvement?

Case 11: Incompetent, but Rich

Roosevelt Elementary School, the largest in the state, is a troubled place. The former principal took early retirement. Irate parents have besieged administrators with a variety of complaints, from the quality of the program to the quality of food served in the cafeteria. The school board has placed it on probation for a two-year period.

To date, all principals at Roosevelt were selected from the ranks of experienced assistant principals in the district. A new policy, however, permits recruiting and hiring principals from outside the district and state. A search committee was formed to find a new principal—someone to lead the school out of the wilderness. The largest church in the community has held prayer meetings asking for "wisdom" to guide the work of the committee.

Central office administrators are at a loss. They believe the school cannot be saved, but they are reluctant to fight the community. The compromise is that the school will have two years to prove itself. As part of this agreement, the new principal must be a tough, no-nonsense individual who will "make sure our kids learn."

Administrator Relations with Parents and Community

After newspaper ads, a nationwide search, and much screening, a candidate has been identified with an outstanding record in a rural school serving children in poverty. This individual is appointed principal of Roosevelt, one of 160 schools in the Great City School System. The new principal, Billie Brown, is the sister-in-law of the pastor of the largest church in the community.

Brown's first act is to disband all faculty committees at the school, because she wants to start "fresh." The committees had been meeting voluntarily, beyond the time stipulated in the teachers' union contract. A small group of teachers approaches Brown and asks permission to continue serving on a committee to aid new teachers. These veteran teachers want to coach beginners—on their own time—after school and during planning periods. They note how successful the committee has been. Brown denies the request, explaining that she wants to start "fresh" and view the situation before establishing any committees.

In the first week of October, Brown appoints several parents to a Community Committee to advise her on school policy. At the committee's first meeting, attendees discussed the "Chicago Model" of education administration, which the group interprets as "parents running the school," including appointing new teachers and reappointing and/or changing the principal every two years. This parent group decides to meet weekly and even elects officers, several of whom are members of the church in which Brown's brother-in-law is the pastor.

During the first semester of the school year, all decision making seems to devolve to Brown. With no standing committees of teachers, Brown and her assistants handle all curriculum, disciplinary, and budget matters. Brown's only input was from the Community Committee: she asked committee members to make recommendations on how the budget should be spent and allocated funds as they directed.

Prior to Christmas, Brown decides that a teacher should serve on the Community Committee. She circulates a memo to faculty members outlining a procedure for electing one teacher representative. The first step calls for a slate of teachers to be nominated. When teachers return their ballots, they are all blank. No teacher agrees to be nominated or serve on the Community Committee. Brown then appoints a teacher, Monica Woods, as the committee's teacher representative. Woods, a beginning teacher with a probationary license, is not a permanent staff member at Roosevelt.

By January, it becomes clear to the Great Cities administration that the school is not improving; indeed, many things are worse. Attendance is down, while complaints and grievances soar among teachers and staff members. Police also are reporting more problems, including break-ins and thefts. Central office supervisors who recently visited Roosevelt report a deterioration of morale and in-school climate. These reports—all oral—provide numerous examples of a school in chaos.

In February, central office administrators hold a full-day evaluation of Brown's activities without informing her and recommend to the superintendent that the principal be removed "as soon as possible, for the good of the school." The superintendent reads the report, interviews his top aides, and informs Brown on the first day of March that she no longer serves as principal of Roosevelt Elementary School. She is suspended with pay pending a full investigation and evaluation. Brown retains a prominent attorney and files suit against the school board for depriving her of due process and her right to pursue a livelihood.

Analysis

Ms. Brown was an authoritarian administrator pursuing autocratic policies. She was insensitive to her role as the leader of the instructional staff, and her vision of leadership dictated that all decision making remain concentrated in the principal's office. She did not understand that, by holding that power, she would also be held accountable when conditions worsened.

By design or accident, Brown succeeded in building a support base among the most powerful community group, which enabled her to dominate the situation. The Great Cities administration and school board had already demonstrated weakness by capitulating to this powerful group on two previous occasions. First, they gave Roosevelt Elementary School two more years of probation despite years of evidence that the school should be closed. Second, they permitted the community group to handpick "one of their own" as the next school principal. Whether Brown was an adept Machiavellian who purposely attached herself to this particular power base or a bumpkin fortunate enough to be employed by a system that did not follow procedures remains unimportant. What matters is that Brown had the support of this community group, and the school system did not provide due process. The issue of due process, rather than Brown's ineffectiveness as a principal whose incompetence hurt students, is what the courts considered.

Procedures requiring lengthy written evaluations must be filed in sequence to remove a principal. At certain points, Brown should be notified of these evaluations, the criteria used, and the conditions under which these criteria would be applied. In many urban school systems, these procedures are typically ignored. Instead, the parties arrive at some "settlement," which means either early retirement or a transfer to a central office job at a higher salary. These settlements obscure the fact that central office administrators have not successfully followed all the procedures for evaluating the school principal. In the whirlwind of running a major school system, administrators and school superintendents often neglect their own homework. They assume—incorrectly—that a principal can just be terminated. By the time they learn that removing a principal is not so simple, it is often too late to follow the paperwork, procedures, and timelines in proper sequence. Consequently, they settle most of these types of cases. In this case, the superintendent and administrators became so focused on Brown's incompetence and autocratic behavior that they behaved in the same way. Her incompetence as a principal does not mean she has lost her rights to due process.

This case also is about community power. The Community Committee essentially did not have the power to make anything good happen at Roosevelt, but it did have the power to prevent progress. School communities involve multiple constituencies frequently at odds. Everyone has a brake—no one has a motor. Every constituency can stop progress, but no single group can make the school work without involving all the others. In this case, the notion that the most powerful community group will improve the school proved untrue and naive. There are many situations in which a powerful group of parents can, for whatever reasons, make a bad school even worse.

If Brown had been competent, she first would have built on the strengths of the situation at Roosevelt. Teachers volunteering their time and effort should have been rewarded and encouraged. By respecting and recognizing such effort, the new principal could have helped shape such teacher activities. Instead, Brown set up a powerful community group in opposition to teachers and then sided with that group. Through poor school administration, Brown established an excellent personal power base.

The courts awarded Brown a $1 million settlement. The central office administrators and superintendent who mishandled the matter were not personally or professionally damaged for their incompetence. Indeed, they enlarged on their incompetence by informing the school it would have to pay off the settlement over a five-year period. When the next principal is assigned, that individual must begin to establish a set of common purposes among the internal and external constituencies. It will be a formidable task.

Chapter 12

Discussion Questions

1. Specifically, what do star principals hope to gain from interacting with parents and caregivers?
2. What and who determines whether community power is being used for beneficial or nefarious purposes?
3. What are the pros and cons of "going outside" to appoint principals in large urban school districts?

A Final Note

The preceding chapters have highlighted a wide range of issues affecting urban schools. Urban educators must sensitize themselves to these issues. Will educators recognize that the ideology of unemployment cited in this book is really being taught in urban schools? Second, will those involved agree to stop supporting the spread of this ideology? This commitment will mean some honest, lengthy meetings among staff members, parents, and students to develop a new set of work goals for the school. Before the third step of teaching genuine work values can be implemented, a school will have to spend a full year or more on the second step of trying to stop teaching the current ideology.

Urban schools are not, in general, involved in teaching and learning. Their primary activity is fighting a war of socialization. Will educators socialize students to the world of work, or will students continue to socialize educators into a culture of nonwork? At present, it is no contest. Urban youth and street values clearly act as the dominant force.

For an urban school to contravene the unstated but effective curriculum of unemployment training successfully, it must have a school leader who understands what is really being taught in the school. The eleven principles presented in this volume will assist a principal who holds the star ideology outlined in the introduction to make a start. He or she must then select an able staff and integrate the efforts of other health and human-service professionals with those of parents and caregivers. It is a formidable challenge, yet one that we dare not miss. The future for the children in these schools depends on our success. Every chaotic school district has several successful schools and the potential for many more. The challenge we face is to establish what star urban principals know as the knowledge base for preparing others. That knowledge is key to the success of children in poverty.

References

Alexander, G. C. 1992. The transformation of an urban principal: Uncertain times, uncertain roles. Paper presented at the annual meeting of the American Educational Research Association, San Francisco, 20–24 April. ERIC ED 348 461.

Bartell, J. F. 1992. Staring from scratch. *Principal* 72(2): 13–14.

Beaumont, J. J. 1997. Issues in urban school district leadership: Professional development. *Urban Education* 31(5): 564–81.

Cohn, K. C., and R. C. Sweeney. 1992. Principal mentoring programs: Are school districts providing the leadership? Paper presented at the annual meeting of the American Educational Research Association, San Francisco, 20–24 April. ERIC ED 345 376.

Cross, R. 1983. Down from the ivory tower: A principal returns to the principalship. *Principal* 62(4): 18–22.

De Angelis, K., and R. Rossi. 1997. Programs for aspiring principals: Who participates? Washington, D.C.: National Center for Education Statistics. ERIC ED 405 644.

Delgadillo, F. 1992. A qualitative analysis of an action research masters program. Ph.D. diss., University of Wisconsin—Milwaukee.

Dill, V. S. 1999. *A peaceable school.* Bloomington, Ind.: Phi Delta Kappa.

Downey, T. 1993. Toward a future for America's children. *Urban Institute Update* (April): 2.

Englert, R. M. 1993. Understanding the urban context and conditions of practice of school administration. Publication series #93–7. Philadelphia: Temple University. ERIC ED 399 310.

Haberman, M. 1982. The legacy of teacher education, 1880–2000. Paper presented at the annual meeting of the American Association of Colleges for Teacher Education, Houston, 17–20 February. ERIC ED 212 575.

Haberman, M. 1987. Recruiting and selecting teachers for urban schools. *ERIC/CUE Urban Diversity Series*, Number 95. ERIC ED 292 942.

Haberman, M. 1994. Gentle teaching in a violent society. *Educational Horizons* 72(3): 131–35.

Haberman, M. 1995. *Star teachers of children in poverty.* West Lafayette, Ind.: Kappa Delta Pi, an International Honor Society in Education.

Haberman, M. 1997. Unemployment training: The ideology of nonwork learned in urban schools. *Phi Delta Kappan* 78(7): 499–503.

Haberman, M. 1999. The anti-learning curriculum of urban schools, Part 2: The solution. *Kappa Delta Pi Record* 35(2): 71–74.

Haberman, H., and G. W. Bracey. 1997. The anti-learning curriculum of urban schools, Part 1: The problem. *Kappa Delta Pi Record* 33(3): 88–89.

Haberman, M., and V. S. Dill. 1995. Commitment to violence among teenagers in poverty. *Kappa Delta Pi Record* 31(4): 148–56.

Haller, E. J., B. O. Brent, and J. H. McNamara. 1994. Does graduate training in educational administration improve America's schools? Another look at some national data. Paper presented at the annual meeting of the American Educational Research Association, New Orleans, 4–8 April. ERIC ED 374 514.

Haller, E. J., B. O. Brent, and J. H. McNamara. 1997. Does graduate training in educational administration improve America's schools? *Phi Delta Kappan* 79(3): 222–27.

Hills, R. J. 1975. The preparation of administrators: Some observations from the firing line. *Educational Administration Quarterly* 11(3): 1–20.

Lem, R. W. 1989. Perceptions of school administrators and professors of education administration regarding the relevance and effectiveness of administrator preparation programs. Ed.D. diss., University of San Francisco.

Lortie, D. C. 1975. *Schoolteacher: A sociological study*. Chicago: University of Chicago Press.

National Center for Education Statistics. 1995. The pocket condition of education. Washington, D.C.: NCES. ERIC ED 386 820.

Pavan, B. N., and N. A. Reid. 1991. Espoused theoretical frameworks and the leadership behaviors of principals in achieving urban elementary schools. Paper presented at the annual meeting of the American Educational Research Association, Chicago, 3–7 April. ERIC ED 337 533.

Payne, C. M. 1984. *Getting what we ask for: The ambiguity of success and failure in urban education*. Westport, Conn.: Greenwood Press.

Pechman, E. M., and J. A. King. 1993. Obstacles to restructuring: Experiences of six middle-grades schools. New York: Teachers College, Columbia University. ERIC ED 362 985.

Wildman, L. 1991. Does the doctorate make a difference? Paper presented at the annual meeting of the National Conference of Professors of Educational Administration, Fargo, N.D., August. ERIC ED 336 827.

Index

persistence of principals, commitment to tasks, 32, instructional leadership, 44–45

positive school climates, counteracting violence, 52–54

poverty, pedagogy of, 21–24; star principals and pedagogy, 24–25

power, basis of gaining respect, 6–7, community/parent relations case study, 92–96; sources of principals' authority, 16–17; use of authority, 17–18

principals, accountability, see accountability of principals; appointing, criteria, xii–xvi; sources of stress, 43, see also star principals

principles of leadership, 29–31

principles of serving the constituency, 31–32; case study, 32–35

project method of teaching, 24–25

projectitis, 81–82; resisting, 84

race, leadership case study, 18–20; parent/community relations, 89

relations with parents and community, 88; case study, 92–96; checklist for school response to community, 91–92; demonstrating respect, 88–89; finding balance among the various voices, 89–91; home visits case study, 38–42; implementing change, case study, 84–87; race/ethnicity/class, 89

respect, demonstrating with parents and community, 88–89; "Respect" value of students, 6–7

serving the constituency, principles of, 31–32; case study, 32–35

star principals, definition of, x–xi; ideology, xi–xii; ideology development, 75; selecting, xi

stress, sources of for principals, 43

subject matter, relevance of, 10–11

success, students' explanations of, 10

superintendent turnover, dealing with, 82–83

tardiness, excuses for, 4–5

teachers; evaluating, 61–62, selecting, 45–46

team building, 32

training of principals in educational administration, 75–76

unity of purpose in serving the constituency, 31–32

urban schools, pedagogy, 21–24; projectitis, 81–82; dealing with superintendent turnover, 82–83; star principals and pedagogy, 24–25; unemployment ideology, see ideology of unemployment

violence in schools, 50; case study, 54–58; counteracting, 52–54; student survey, 51–52

workload management due to new projects, 84